The Allure of
TURQUOISE

NEW MEXICO
MAGAZINE

Many Navajo people such as this man outside his hogan in the late 1930s wore most of their collection of jewelry as a symbol of wealth. (*New Mexico Magazine* Archival Collection, photographer unknown)

© 2005 by *New Mexico Magazine*
Published 2005

18   17   16   15   14   13   2   3   4   5   6   7

ISBN-10: 0-937206-87-3
ISBN-13: 978-0-937206-87-4

Library of Congress Control Number: 2005926152

New Mexico Magazine
495 Old Santa Fe Trail, Santa Fe, New Mexico 87501

Special thanks to the folks at The Turquoise Museum in Albuquerque for all of their valuable help in the research of this project.

Front and back cover: A conglomerate of turquoise stones illustrates many varieties of the mineral. (Photo by Mark Nohl)

Printed in China

The top Pueblo cross necklace, circa 1900, is made of coin silver. The outer squash blossom necklace, circa 1890-1910, is set with green Cerrillos turquoise stone that used to be in an ear bob. (Necklaces courtesy of Morning Star Gallery, Santa Fe)

TABLE OF CONTENTS

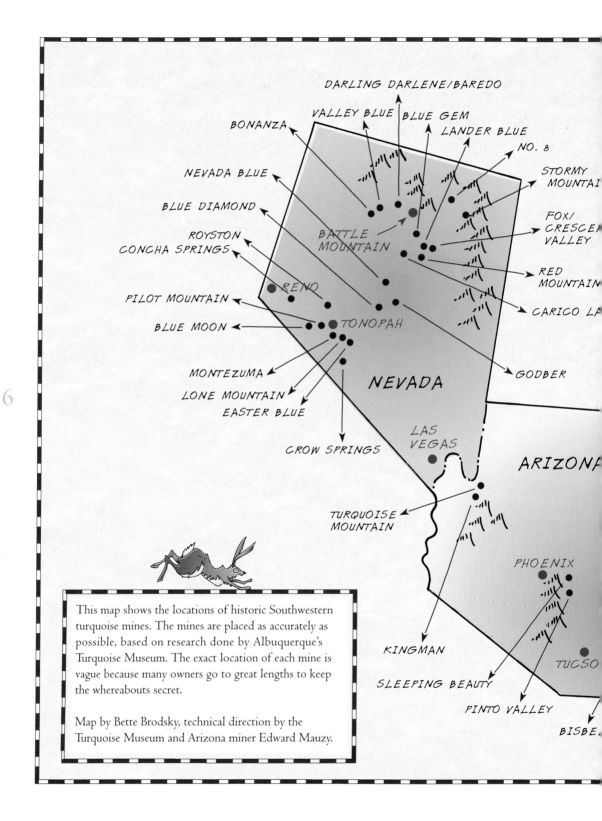

DARLING DARLENE/BAREDO

VALLEY BLUE   BLUE GEM

BONANZA   LANDER BLUE

NO. 8

NEVADA BLUE   STORMY MOUNTAI

BLUE DIAMOND   FOX/ CRESCE VALLEY

ROYSTON
CONCHA SPRINGS

BATTLE MOUNTAIN

RED MOUNTAIN

RENO

PILOT MOUNTAIN   CARICO LA

BLUE MOON   TONOPAH

MONTEZUMA   NEVADA   GODBER

LONE MOUNTAIN

EASTER BLUE

LAS VEGAS

CROW SPRINGS   ARIZONA

TURQUOISE MOUNTAIN

PHOENIX

KINGMAN   TUCSO

SLEEPING BEAUTY

PINTO VALLEY

BISBE

6

This map shows the locations of historic Southwestern turquoise mines. The mines are placed as accurately as possible, based on research done by Albuquerque's Turquoise Museum. The exact location of each mine is vague because many owners go to great lengths to keep the whereabouts secret.

Map by Bette Brodsky, technical direction by the Turquoise Museum and Arizona miner Edward Mauzy.

TURQUOISE MINES
OF THE SOUTHWEST

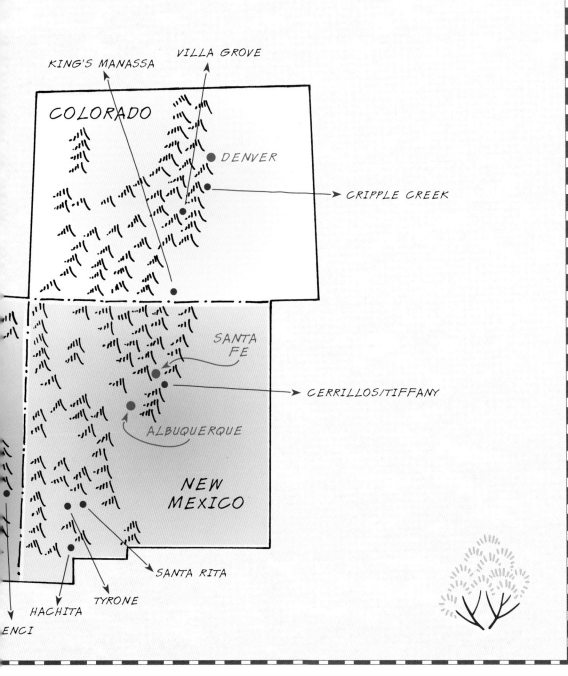

KING'S MANASSA

VILLA GROVE

COLORADO

● DENVER

➤ CRIPPLE CREEK

SANTA FE

➤ CERRILLOS/TIFFANY

ALBUQUERQUE

NEW MEXICO

➤ SANTA RITA

TYRONE

HACHITA

ENCI

In the spirit of prehistoric style, Mary Agnes Garcia of Santo Domingo Pueblo combined Kingman turquoise and spiny oyster shells to create this stunning necklace. (Necklace courtesy of Wadle Galleries, Santa Fe)

EXPLORING THE MIRACLE OF TURQUOISE

BY SUSAN ARRITT

So many geologic chains of events must synchronize to create just one thin vein of turquoise that the mineral can rightly be envisioned as a fluke of nature.

It is not an abundant, run-of-the-mill mineral, as one might gather from the vast inventories of blues and greens that fill marketplaces throughout New Mexico. Rather, turquoise is the rare and improbable product of an incalculable number of chemical and physical processes that must take place in the right combination and proper environment over a time span of hundreds of thousands — if not millions — of years.

Turquoise occurs almost exclusively in arid lands. In North America, it is most abundant in dry, copper-rich regions of the southwestern United States — Nevada, Colorado, Arizona and New Mexico — where it has been mined aggressively since prehistoric times. The blue-green mineral also occurs sporadically in the Mexican states of Sonora and Zacatecas, California's Mojave Desert, western Texas and Utah. And, rare deposits that defy the gem's usual propensity for desert conditions are found in the humid climates of Alabama and in southern Virginia, site of the world's only known turquoise crystals. Elsewhere on the planet, deposits of turquoise are native to Peru, Australia, Turkestan, Iran (formerly Persia), Siberia, China, Ethiopia, France, Germany and the Sinai Peninsula, where the oldest known turquoise mines were operated by the Egyptians as early as 5500 B.C. Today, turquoise mines are in Iran, China and in the American Southwest.

In the raw, this world-renowned gemstone is found at high elevations and is almost never deeper than 100 feet below the surface of the earth. There, for millennia, wind and water slowly chisel away at the landscape's rocky outcroppings, causing the erosion of particles that contain elements such as iron, copper and phosphorus, the latter two of which are key components in turquoise. These and other minerals eventually dissolve and percolate through the surrounding rocks, making their way through the labyrinthine fissures, crevices and holes of what are called mother rocks or host rocks — the sites where turquoise will form. Although these may be metamorphic rocks such as gneisses or schists — or sedimentary, like shales or sandstones — mother rocks are most often fractured igneous (volcanic) rocks. In the turquoise-bearing regions of the American Southwest, including New Mexico, common mother rocks include granite, trachyte and monzonite porphyry, all of which are igneous in origin.

Long before this rainwater-turned-groundwater infiltrated the mother rocks, however, far more intense chemical activity had been well under way far below the cavernous mazes. Chemical elements, such as phosphorus, sulfur and aluminum, had long been brewing intensively with rising gases and steam. According to Cornelis Klein, a University of New Mexico professor of Earth and Planetary Sciences in the 1990s, such mineral-rich hydrothermal fluids and associated igneous activity were responsible for the original formation of copper sulfides and pyrite (an iron sulfide) as well as apatite (a calcium phosphate). These minerals, present in earlier copper-iron sulfide ore deposits or as apatite grains in igneous rocks, were the primary source materials that were attacked by subsequent weathering and oxidation.

In the slow weathering process the descending groundwater continually interacted with the original source minerals and recombined the elements necessary for the formation of turquoise (that is, copper, aluminum, phosphorus and hydroxyl-OH-groups) as deposits along fractures and cavities in the mother rock (the host rock).

If there is too much descending groundwater — as in regions with humid climates — the elements crucial to turquoise production will be flushed away. Or, if there is too little of one element or too much of another, the perfect concoction for turquoise will not evolve. But in those long-shot situations when conditions are ideal, the mineral-rich solutions deposited in the nooks and crannies of the host rock eventually harden into veins or nodules of the turquoise mineral. This precious gem of blue and green is, technically, a hydrated basic aluminum and copper phosphate. The typical scientific formula is $CuAl_6(PO_4)_4(OH)_8 \cdot 5H_2O$.

Pueblo Indian legend says that turquoise steals its blue color from the sky. Geologists, on the other hand, attribute a stone's degree of blueness to the amount of copper present in the deposits that occur in holes and faults in the mother rock. The deeper the shade of blue, the higher the copper concentration. Iron, too, influences the color of turquoise, turning it varied shades of green. While the mineral is forming, iron might replace some of the copper, which results in increasingly darker shades of green as the metal content rises.

Turquoise taken directly from the ground contains water and, therefore, retains a deep hue. But when exposed to the air, the blue-green stone turns a lighter shade as moisture is drawn from it through the process of evaporation. The most porous and low-grade forms of turquoise, called "chalk," might even turn bone white when depleted of water.

Jimmy Bailon used several types of turquoise in these interesting necklaces. The innermost necklace features a Darling Darlene bead and coral heishi. Then come pieces composed of Carico Lake, Red Mountain, Sleeping Beauty and Blue Gem beads.

Both of these classic squash blossom necklaces herald Blue Gem turquoise stones from Nevada. The top necklace is by Vickie Martine. (Jewelry courtesy of the Turquoise Museum)

Around the world, chalk is the most prevalent form of turquoise, accounting for more than 90 percent of all the mineral that is mined today. It is too soft to polish, nearly impossible to cut without crumbling, and aesthetically unappealing to most Western eyes. Yet chalk is easily dyed, stabilized with resins, injected with plastics and otherwise treated so that it is hard and workable, saleable and even beautiful.

In the Southwest, the darker shades of blue and green turquoise are considered the highest grades. Generally, the deeper and richer the color, the harder the nugget and the more easily it will polish to a high luster, an important determinant of gem quality. In other cultures, pale shades of turquoise command top price.

The most treasured Persian turquoise, for example, is solid, or clear, robin's egg blue and adorns gold jewelry and art treasures in Iran and elsewhere in the Middle East. Light-colored and seemingly radiant, this turquoise-of-choice traditionally would be edged out here by the hardier-looking, matrix-laden gemstones that reign in popularity in the Land of Enchantment. The fact that Persian turquoise includes not a hint of matrix, or foreign matter, boosts its homeland market value tremendously. Not so on this side of the Atlantic, however.

"Matrix" is practically the requisite buzzword for Southwestern turquoise aficionados these days. The bolder the better, they say, in reference to the extraneous matter that is incorporated in many turquoise deposits early on, then becomes permanently enmeshed in the final hardened vein of blue or green. The matrix, which might be red, white, black, brown, golden or even lavender, is usually part of the mother rock that surrounds the subterranean mineral deposit. Often, veins of turquoise are so thin (sometimes only half an inch at their widest point) that removing them from a mine almost always means bringing along parts of the host wall in the process, whether miners use explosives, ride-on excavating equipment or merely a pickax.

Other times, fingerlike igneous rock projections jut into the holes and crevices filled with turquoise deposits. These, plus other sorts of foreign minerals such as quartz, limonite, kaolinite, hematite and clay — which might have been leached from nearby rock formations — entwine themselves like arteries throughout the turquoise during its deposition. And some pyrite may add a distinctive shimmer of "fool's gold" to the gem.

Today, the most highly-desired matrix pattern is the spiderweb, which resembles highly detailed netting that envelopes the mineral, inside and out. Nevada's No. 8 Mine, a onetime gold and copper mining operation on the west side of the Tuscarora Mountain Range, has produced one of the most prized spiderweb turquoise deposits in the world. Deep blue nodules of the mineral lie in the folds and faults of black chert and quartz veins. Among the most valuable specimens brought up from No. 8 was a 150-pound nodule, which, like many from the mine, was an intense, dark blue that appeared draped with a crocheted black netting.

Web matrix has a netlike pattern that is less precisely defined than spiderweb, yet its strands are still generally connected. And, finally, matrix turquoise is the least valuable and most prevalent of the three, with random and only occasionally connected veins of minerals running through it. Sometimes swirls of varied shades of green or blue will appear to be some sort of matrix in themselves. Such irregularities, which are often quite stunning enhancements, are merely evidence that some original minerals in the underground aqueous solution did not mix well early on.

New Mexico's gem-quality turquoise is world renowned. It occurs in a wondrous palette of colors and matrices, as was observed in 1907 by geologist Edward Zaienski who wrote of the broad array of natural specimens from one area in southwestern New Mexico.

From prehistoric times until the early 20th century, New Mexico was this continent's forerunner in turquoise extraction. Most of its mines lay within a wedge bounded roughly by the four most prominent turquoise mining sites: the Cerrillos Hills near Santa Fe; the Jarilla Mountains, north of Orogrande; the Little Hatchet Mountains, west of Hachita; and the Burro Mountains, southwest of Tyrone.

The Burro Mountains, where "Turquoise John" Coleman staked the region's first modern-day claim in 1875, are primarily composed of granite and quartz, through which run turquoise veins and nuggets. Most significant of its sites is the Azure Mine, southwest of Silver City, which was the location of the renowned "Elizabeth Pocket." In the 1915 National Academy of Sciences publication, *The Turquois* (sic), author Joseph E. Pogue writes that, at the time, the Azure Mine had been operated "more extensively than any other turquois (sic) mine in this country." The book, now updated, remains the classic reference book in its field.

Since the mineral occurs so close to the surface, the Azure Mine was predominantly an open-pit operation. The turquoise deposit, wrote Pogue, measured "about 600 feet in length, 100 to 200 feet in width, and 60 feet in depth, with tunnels at several levels." Its Elizabeth Pocket, with stones of "translucent, deep blue," yielded "more high-quality turquois (sic) than any single deposit on record." Estimates of the mine's total production at the time ranged from $2 million to $4 million.

Not far away, miners of the 1880s hoped to find gold in the hillsides of the Little Hatchet Mountains, near Hachita. Like prehistoric peoples had long ago discovered, though, this region of volcanic rocks, sandstone and slate was also rich in turquoise. The gem-quality stones ran the gamut from pale blue to greenish blue. At the Cameo claim could be found

Royston turquoise necklace by Ava Marie Coriz of Santo Domingo Pueblo. (Necklace courtesy of Wadle Galleries, Santa Fe)

Using only Kingman turquoise, Mary Agnes Garcia created this traditional style necklace. (Necklace courtesy of Wadle Galleries, Santa Fe)

some of the best specimens in the region; they were generally pure blue and were cut into cameos. The mine later operated as an open-pit turquoise extraction operation and, despite rumors to the contrary, is reportedly only used occasionally for the extraction of low-grade chalk from tailings.

To the east, in the Jarilla Mountains north of Orogrande, traces of turquoise can still be found. Indigenous peoples mined

Above: Rare Cerrillos turquoise stones adorn these two bracelets and ring, Navajo-made before the 1920s. (Jewelry courtesy of the Turquoise Museum)

Below: Sky Horse spiderweb turquoise all the way from China adorn these pieces made by Leonard Platero. (Jewelry courtesy of the Turquoise Museum)

this locale long before Europeans staked claims in this region. Now long abandoned, the most recent operations began in 1892, when turquoise was discovered in crevices of trachyte along the entire length of a 70-foot mine shaft. And, close to the ground surface, it appeared among deposits of limonite, gypsum, and kaolin as clumpy nodules of green and blue that faded quickly once exposed to the air above ground.

The northernmost region for turquoise mining in New Mexico was in the Cerrillos District, just south of Santa Fe. From prehistoric times through the early part of the 20th century, this was the most acclaimed region on the continent for turquoise production. Turquoise from the Cerrillos deposits on Mount Chalchihuitl

and Turquoise Hill forms in nodules and extremely thin veins. Colors vary from dark green to blue-green and bright to pale blues. Shimmering pyrite is sometimes intermingled in the typical Chalchihuitl matrix of monzonite and latite, and it is often naturally stained with brown limonite. For its size and yield — more than $2 million worth was extracted by the American Turquoise Co. — the Tiffany Mine at Turquoise Hill reportedly produced the greatest percentage of gem-quality turquoise in the nation near the turn of the century.

In the late 1960s and throughout the '70s, the United States was struck with "turquoise fever." Jewelry with the blue-green gemstone was all the rage across the nation, and demand for it soared after *The Wall Street Journal* declared turquoise to be on par with diamonds as one of the hottest investment bets! As still is the case, New Mexico continued to rank as the nation's top center for the cutting and crafting of the stone. But of the numerous mining operations

The box pendant (upper left) features a stone from Turquoise Mountain, while the deep-blue nugget (lower left) is Morenci turquoise from Arizona. The chained pendant (middle) uses Lone Mountain turquoise from Nevada and the John Charlie bracelet (far right) hosts Kingman turquoise from Arizona. (Jewelry courtesy of the Turquoise Museum)

A mine in Tyrone, N.M., provided the turquoise stones for this 14-karat gold over sterling silver bracelet and ring made by Luke Billy Yazzie. (Jewelry courtesy of the Turquoise Museum)

or claims that dotted the state at the time, none were producing any noteworthy quantities, as were mines in neighboring states. Output from the 150 or more mines elsewhere in the Southwest was at an all-time high.

Late in the 1800s, mining operations in Colorado, Nevada and Arizona began to catch up with the prolific yields of mines in New Mexico. Soon after the turn of the century, Nevada, with its rich north-south belt of mineralization, became the nation's No. 1 producer of turquoise. Besides the famed No. 8 mine, this region is home to Lone Mountain Mine, with its high-quality web turquoise, and Blue Gem Mine, which has produced an alluring, dark blue gem that almost appears to be dyed by human hands. One of the most popular and expensive kinds of turquoise in the 1960s and '70s came from Nevada's Lander Blue Mine, which produced small nuggets of "blue blue" turquoise with a tiny black spiderweb matrix.

In Colorado, turquoise was primarily found in the same mountainous areas that were favored by gold and silver miners during the 1880s. Places such as King's Manassa, Cripple

Creek and Leadville produced respectable yields of gem-quality turquoise, but none was finer or more valuable than the deposits mined near Villa Grove.

Arizona is home to three of the most famous and prolific turquoise production areas — the open-pit copper mines at Kingman, Bisbee and Morenci. There, turquoise has actually always been a secondary product. Specific turquoise mining rights were paid to take out the blue-green gem. But some, like the so-called "lunch bucket boys," hid bootleg nuggets in their lunch pails and sold them privately on the sly.

Today, only one mine in the entire Southwest is reportedly producing any commercially viable quantities of gem-quality natural turquoise that does not need to be stabilized or otherwise treated. At the Sleeping Beauty Mine, in the Globe-Miami area east of Phoenix, an estimated 500 to 1,000 pounds a year are still pulled from the ground. Similar in color to the clear blue of Kingman turquoise, that from Sleeping Beauty is soft enough to be sliced so that it has less matrix and a uniformity of color.

Throughout New Mexico and the Southwest, there is little other turquoise mining activity other than the "Sunday miners," or hobbyists. Still, rumors fly about highly prosperous (yet, of course, secret) goings-on in the most remote of the old mines around the state.

Most turquoise mines in New Mexico and throughout the Southwest have been either played out, or have just bitten the dust for financial reasons. Some blame strict occupational safety regulations. Others point to the $50,000 to $100,000 cash bonds that must be paid in advance to ensure that land and vegetation are reclaimed. But whatever the reasons, turquoise is enjoying such a resurgence in popularity that most of the gems recently in New Mexico's $2 billion dollar turquoise industry come from China, where there is such a glutted market that both natural and stabilized stones can cost the wholesale buyer roughly the same price.

Susan Arritt has written and edited extensively on the natural sciences. She is a former writer for the United Nations International fund for Agricultural Development in Rome.

Spiderweb turquoise accentuates these pieces, including earrings by Luke Billy Yazzie (upper left and right), a bracelet by Kathy Abeita (lower left), a necklace and bracelet by an unknown artist (upper center-right), Lander blue turquoise rings by Joe Chee (center), and a Lone Mountain turquoise bracelet by Johnny Pablo (lower right). (Jewelry courtesy of the Turquoise Museum)

Intricate Carico Lake turquoise decorates this impressive grizzly bear skull from the collection of Gus's Trading Co. in Albuquerque.

THE ALLURE OF TURQUOISE THROUGH THE CENTURIES

BY MARK SIMMONS

When the New Mexico Legislature adopted turquoise as the state gem in 1967, it officially acknowledged the importance of "the sky blue stone" in the culture and history of Southwestern peoples.

Perhaps in the popular mind, nothing is more emblematic of the Land of Enchantment than a piece of turquoise jewelry. Few are the visitors who can resist acquiring a sample or two.

The word turquoise comes to us from French and means Turkish stone, seemingly because the mineral was first introduced to Western Europe from Persia, by way of Turkey. But the Moors of Spain also delighted in the use of turquoise, their source being North Africa where the ancient Egyptians knew of it as early as the fourth century B.C. In Spanish, the word is *turquesa*.

Among the Indians of the Southwest, turquoise was used for religious and ornamental purposes. For the Navajos it once passed as currency. Apaches liked to attach a small piece to the bow so that their arrows would fly true. The Zunis of western New Mexico valued it most of all — a string of turquoise beads was formerly worth several horses.

In Zuni tradition, the rich blue color of the stone symbolizes "the supreme life-giving power," and fragments of turquoise are used for the eyes of fetishes and are commingled with sacred corn meal and presented as an offering to masked deities. Most tribes believe that turquoise brings good fortune and ensures a long and healthful life, hence its age-old popularity as a personal ornament.

In New Mexico, the Indians for centuries extracted the gem from the Cerrillos Hills a few miles south of Santa Fe. This was the site, in fact, of the most extensive prehistoric mining operation in America, containing as it did the largest known deposit of turquoise on the continent.

At the center of these hills rises Mount Chalchihuitl where aboriginal workers carved out a pit from solid rock measuring 200 feet in depth and resulting in the removal of 100,000 tons of waste rock. This feat appears truly marvelous as we observe that it was accomplished with stone axes, mauls, picks and chisels.

Left: Potsherds and crude stone mauls used in turquoise extraction still litter the tailings debris at the Tiffany Mine.

Near the quarry also can be found, to this day, vertical shafts and tunnels. Access was gained by use of notched logs, known as chicken ladders. Indian miners would climb these, hand-over-hand, bearing leather buckets of broken rock on their shoulders or backs.

The term *chalchihuitl* derives from the word *xiuitle*, signifying "turquoise" in the Aztec language. Spaniards and their Aztec servants introduced it to the area from central Mexico.

Cerrillos turquoise gained fame far and wide among Native Americans, both for its abundance and richness of color. As an article of trade, it found its way into the southeastern United States, northward into Canada and as far south as middle Mexico and the Mayan homeland. Legend has it that Aztec emperor Montezuma bedecked himself in necklaces and pendants of turquoise from the remote Cerrillos mines. At prehistoric Pueblo Bonito in New Mexico's Chaco Canyon, archaeologists have recovered some 50,000 pieces of turquoise, more than half of it in the form of beads.

The pueblo of San Marcos, founded about 1300 just east of the Cerrillos hills, soon laid claim to the old mine workings. Its residents jealously guarded the entrance to the turquoise deposits and Indians coming from distant places to gather the stone were obliged to seek their permission. Having control of such a valuable resource, San Marcos prospered.

In 1535 the wandering Spaniard Cabeza de Vaca, with several companions, passed through the desert south of El Paso. Communicating with the local Indians by signs, they learned of the Pueblo people living on the great river to the north who wore cotton clothes and jewelry of blue stone. This was the first report of New Mexico's famous turquoise.

Five years later, the explorer Francisco Vázquez de Coronado found an abundance of turquoise ornaments among the Indians of Zuni and Pecos pueblos. But the semiprecious

The sun shines through the entrance of the Tiffany Mine near Cerrillos and lights up the inner shaft. This mine and many others in the area have been worked for centuries.

A well-worn path leads to the entrance of the Tiffany Mine. The site has served as backdrop for the movie *Lucky Luke* and the television series *Earth 2*.

stone held little interest for him since he was intent upon finding the fabled Golden Cities of Cíbola. Some of the specimens he did collect, however, are rumored to have been sent across the Atlantic to enrich the crown jewels of Spain.

Of the later Spanish interest in turquoise, Susan Wallace, wife of territorial governor Lew Wallace, wrote: "Tradition is that in colonial days Indian slaves worked the Chalchihuitl mines under the lash of the conqueror. In 1680, by accident, a portion of the rock fell and killed thirty Pueblos (Pueblo Indians). The Spaniards immediately made a requisition on the town of San Marcos for more natives to take their places."

That incident, she claims, touched off the terrible Pueblo Revolt of 1680, resulting in the deaths of 400 colonists and expulsion of the rest from New Mexico. The Indians promptly concealed the turquoise mines and thereafter kept their locations secret. Her little story, often told by others as well, must be classed as folklore, because absolutely nothing exists in the historical record to confirm it.

Indeed, Pueblo Indians quietly continued to extract turquoise from the Cerrillos deposits until the 1870s, when a silver mining boom suddenly enveloped the district. Prospectors noted the old quarries and wondered if the blue stone might not be commercially profitable.

Santa Fe businessmen and politicians, including Wallace, entered into schemes to gain control and exploit the most promising turquoise claims. Together with Eastern investors they formed syndicates and drew up elaborate development plans. As in any speculative venture, a few persons made substantial profits, while others suffered losses and disappointment.

One difficulty arose from litigation growing out of claims dating back to a Spanish land grant of 1728. Another appeared when the Tiffany Co. of New York, after investing some $100,000 in exploration, discovered that the oldest and most famous turquoise digging on Mount Chalchihuitl had been largely exhausted by the Indians and contained little marketable stone.

Hurculano Montoya of La Cienega works the Tiffany Mine sometime in the latter 1930s, nearly a decade before the last known turquoise was removed from the Cerrillos-area mines. (Historical photo by Bill Lippincott, Sallie Wagner Collection, Museum of New Mexico Neg. No. 5236)

But on the north edge of the district, at Turquoise Hill, rich lodes were revealed and put into production, among them the Castillian Mine dating from colonial days. The North American Turquoise Co. of New York bought up much of this site. Tiffany's, which had a principal interest in the firm, allegedly took out $2 million worth of gem material between 1892 and 1899. Its mining claims on Turquoise Hill had such colorful names as Blue Bell, Morning Star, Blue Gem and Sky Blue.

While syndicates and affluent politicians had most of the field sewn up within a few years, a few lucky prospectors now and then made a "find" on one of the smaller claims. One

Left: The Spanish worked the Castillian Mine as part of the "Our Lady of the Sorrows" operation before being forced from the area in the Pueblo Revolt of 1680.

of them turned up the largest rough turquoise nugget ever found in the district. Nicknamed "Jumbo," it was a sky blue stone as large as a pigeon's egg.

The color of much of the Cerrillos turquoise was the same deep blue seen in Jumbo. This hue was favored over the greenish turquoise obtained in Grant County and other sites in New Mexico. The stone's main use was for costume jewelry, but pieces of inferior grade were also in demand for inlay work on cabinets and tabletops.

Raw turquoise was packed in boxes and shipped for cutting to jewelry firms in New

York. Very little of it was commercially cut in the territory. We would have to regard the wages paid to miners as far from generous. Hispanic workers averaged $1.50 a day and Anglos got $2.50, an early example of wage discrimination.

The largest mines had need of no more than seven to 10 men and in good rock this force could take out as much as $10,000 worth of gemstone daily. The miners found the best turquoise in nodules surrounded by lime encrustations. It was most stable and less liable to lose its color upon exposure to dry air or to shatter when being cut.

The mine owners attempted to work their claims in complete secrecy, using armed guards to prevent entry of all outsiders. This was done partly to keep potential thieves from getting a look at the diggings. But it also helped in hoodwinking the tax collector. A major quantity of the blue stone left New Mexico unreported, but government officials intercepted one gunnysack containing $50,000 worth of turquoise.

For a while Pueblo Indians persisted in slipping on to the now-private claims and carrying away some of the marginal stone. Nearby Santo Domingo Pueblo, in fact, asserted proprietary rights over the ancient mines because some of its residents were descendants of the now extinct village of San Marcos. In the early 20th century, four Indians of Cochití entered the turquoise workings illegally, were arrested and received prison sentences. That incident discouraged further trespassing.

Toward the end of the last century, several important turquoise mines were discovered and developed in southern New Mexico, although none proved as rich as the Cerrillos District. One of these was the Jarilla Mine in Otero County, not far from Alamogordo and the second was in the Hachita Mining District in the southwestern corner of the territory. A hunter, however, made the largest discovery, in 1875 in the Burro Mountains below Silver City.

Jeweler Charles L. Tiffany and his American Turquoise Co. descended upon the Burros and promptly bought up the new claims. The output was soon reported as larger and of better quality than turquoise from the mines of Persia. The celebrated Elizabeth Pocket in the district yielded the largest amount of high-grade turquoise documented in a single deposit.

By the time the boom in Indian turquoise jewelry came along in the 1960s, most of New Mexico's mines had been exhausted. Native craftspeople buy huge quantities of the stone from other states, principally from Nevada, or from foreign sources. But to many people, New Mexico is still thought of as the Land of Turquoise!

Noted historian Marc Simmons lives in the Cerrillos area and is the author of more than 30 books, including *Treasure Trails of the Southwest* and *When Six-Guns Ruled: Outlaw Tales of the Southwest*.

A turquoise pendant sits inside a prehistoric Glycymeris gigantea shell bracelet. Surrounding the two pieces are Ancestral Pueblo pendants made of (from top left, clockwise) argillite, clay, shell and selenite. (All pieces recovered from Chaco Culture National Historical Park, courtesy of the Maxwel Museum and National Park Service)

TURQUOISE AND THE NATIVE AMERICAN

BY DAVID GOMEZ

Turquoise has significance to New Mexico's Native American people that touches many areas of life, including the spiritual, economic and historic.

At Chaco Canyon, researchers date the earliest turquoise jewelry to between A.D. 500 and 700. Today, Pueblo families and individual craftspeople support themselves through the production and sale of carved animal figures called fetishes and silver and turquoise jewelry. Some use the stone to pray.

"Turquoise has a very profound meaning for us," says Alex Seowtewa, who with his sons Kenneth and Edwin has spent most of the past three decades restoring the murals at the old Our Lady of Guadalupe Church at Zuni. Turquoise fragments saved by Zuni Pueblo jewelers and carvers are often collected by family members, who then make the stone part of their offerings, he says.

"We don't take anything for granted," Seowtewa says. "We pray for a blessed life, a productive life and wish for a beautiful life."

The earliest known association of Native Americans and turquoise in the region actually comes from a site in northeastern Arizona, where it was found in a burial site dating to before A.D. 500, says Frances Joan Mathien, Ph.D., a National Park Service archaeologist associated with the Chaco Project since 1978.

The oldest turquoise pieces from Chaco itself were found at a cluster of pithouses and a kiva known as *Shabik'eshchee* village, she says. At that stage of Chacoan culture, from between A.D. 500 and 700, most of the turquoise pieces found were flakes that might have been attached as a mosaic to wood or baskets that have since disintegrated.

"In the Southwest, as agriculture became more established, you see an increased use of blue-green stones, including turquoise," Mathien says.

As the culture developed, the Ancestral Pueblo of Chaco Canyon began to drill the turquoise and make jewelry for personal use. "The jewelry generally consists of shell bracelets and turquoise necklaces and pendants that would have been used by ordinary people," Mathien says.

The jewelry from later stages of Ancestral Pueblo culture tended not to be associated

Other items collected from Chaco include a necklace of shale, calcite and shell beads adorned with turquoise, shell, gypsite and argillite pendants; a black jet ring; and a carved bird fetish of blackish-red hermatitie.

with burial sites, with one significant exception. "At Pueblo Bonito, there are two men who were buried with 56,000 pieces of turquoise," Mathien says. "On top of them are two wooden boards and several other people, about 16 or 18, who were also buried with turquoise, but not as much. The two men were obviously very important, and there was evidence of battery upon their heads."

Two turquoise mines at Cerrillos near Santa Fe have long been important to the Pueblo people, and some historians believe that the stones might have been traded as far as northern Mexico. While some of the mines' output could have been used by the Ancestral Pueblo, "I doubt that Cerrillos was the only source of turquoise in the prehistoric Southwest," Mathien says. "There are mines in Colorado, southern New Mexico, Arizona, Nevada and California. Until there are many more studies done, I would hesitate to say where the turquoise in Chaco came from."

Another question with no definite answer is what turquoise meant to the Ancestral

Pueblo people. Mathien ventured no opinion on the issue, except to say that the blue-green color may have been more important than the stone itself. Indeed, archaeologists have found pendants made of fake turquoise in the form of blue painted stones that date to about A.D. 900 to 1000, according to E. Wesley Jernigan, author of *Jewelry of the Prehistoric Southwest*.

The Ancestral Pueblo people gradually abandoned Chaco Canyon most likely in the face of drought in the late 1100s, and the people dispersed and established the other villages. Spanish explorers from 1540 on noted the turquoise necklaces, teardrops and earrings worn by the Southwestern natives, pieces that were the subject of later exploration in which the focus was knowledge. Francisco Vázquez de Coronado, who was on a mission to explore the Seven Cities of Cíbola after earlier reports told of a region of great wealth, sent turquoise stones and mosaics on wooden combs back to Viceroy Don Antonio de Mendoza in Mexico. One of the fabled Seven Cities was *Hawikuh*, an early Pueblo site near Zuni. Frederick Hodges excavated turquoise bracelets and necklaces at *Hawikuh* between 1917 and 1920. The archaeologist also found several combs covered in a mosaic of turquoise, jet and coral, which he believed were used prior to 1650. Pitch from the piñon tree provided the adhesive.

Two ancient Ancestral Pueblo turquoise pendants rest on beads used in various pieces of prehistoric jewelry. (All pieces courtesy of the Maxwell Museum and National Park Service)

33

Among New Mexico's Pueblo peoples, the Zuni are regarded as having a noteworthy relationship with turquoise in which the stone is incorporated into nearly all aspects of life, from the sacred to the economic. Turquoise has been a part of Zuni religious practice for hundreds of years. Men representing deities known as kachinas wear turquoise necklaces in dances, as do the unmasked female dancers.

Ground turquoise is often set out as part of an offering, and the stone also adorns ceremonial objects. Some of the turquoise is said to have come from a mine in the Zuni Mountains, but outsiders have not confirmed a location.

Ancestors of today's Zuni people also recognized the importance of major prey animals native to the region, including the mountain lion, wildcat, wolf, coyote, mole and eagle. Figures of these animals were carved from stone or found in nature and carried by hunters. Frank Hamilton Cushing, the ethnologist who lived at Zuni for a number of years in the late 1800s, described what he knew of their meaning and origin in his 1880 report to the Smithsonian Institution, later published under the title *Zuni Fetiches*. Some of the sacred fetishes described by Cushing were adorned with turquoise eyes or nuggets tied to their backs, a practice that continues today in places where they are made for sale to the outside world.

Perhaps the biggest change in the role of turquoise in Zuni life occurred with the introduction of silversmithing, which is credited to a Navajo named Adsidi Chon who moved to Zuni in 1872 after the tribe returned from exile at Bosque Redondo. A Zuni man named Kineshde is said to have been the first at the village to set turquoise into silver jewelry about 1890. That innovation, combined with the influence of traders and collectors such as C.G. Wallace and increased access to gas torches and other tools, set off an artistic and economic movement that continues today. About 1,000 jewelers are now active at Zuni, and whole families are known for their contributions to the continued development of Zuni jewelry.

Fetish carver Dan Simplicio Jr., a former anthropology student at the University of New

Above: Alex Seowtewa of Zuni Pueblo stands beneath a massive mural that he and his sons restored at the church in Zuni Pueblo.

Opposite: A detail of the restored section of the mural inside the Our Lady of Guadalupe Church at Zuni Pueblo.

Mexico in Albuquerque, recalls the team approach to silversmithing used by his late parents, Dan Sr. and Esther.

"He worked for a trading company in Gallup, and she stayed home," Simplicio says. "He would do the silverwork and leave it behind, and go to work the next day. She would set the stones and polish them as well, so by the time he got back those would be finished and he could start on another set."

The elder Simplicio worked with Navajo silversmiths in Gallup, a unique situation that led to an exchange of ideas and techniques. "They were bouncing ideas off each other, and I think they produced some of the greatest pieces of that time," Simplicio says, referring to the 1960s. "A whole different style came out of that, and they were some of the pioneers."

Collectors, including the Heard Museum in Phoenix, prized the Simplicios' work. While his son has tried, mostly unsuccessfully, to obtain some of his parent's work, he has acquired some of his father's sand-casting molds.

"I saw what they did, and I'm certain I can do it, too," Simplicio says. He was still very young when his father died, however, so the self-taught fetish carver started off at a disadvantage. But his stone-working skills helped him make the transition to using turquoise in jewelry, following a long line of jewelers including his great-uncle who learned from Adsidi Chon.

Today, the Zuni jewelry industry is worth several million dollars annually to the pueblo, according to James Ostler of the Pueblo of Zuni Arts and Crafts. "We buy a million dollars worth a year," says Ostler, who notes that the tribal enterprise is but one of many major trading operations at Zuni.

The Zunis' long relationship with turquoise is not likely to change in the near future. "People are not turning away from turquoise," said Marian Rodee, curator of Southwestern Ethnology at the University of New Mexico's Maxwell Museum of Anthropology.

"Younger artists who use other stones still use turquoise," said Rodee, co-author of *Zuni: A Village of Silversmiths*. "When they take orders from people at the pueblo, they still use the traditional materials — coral, shell, jet and turquoise.

"Many of the younger people like some of the smaller art pieces that are meant to be seen close up like on a suit, rather than as a manta pin or as a bow guard," Rodee says. "But in the dress for the dances, there is continued use of cluster work that you can see across the plaza — big, bold work. Good turquoise is highly valued, and is passed from generation to generation like family heirlooms.

"I don't see any changes — it's too deep in their culture."

David Gomez, a native of Taos Pueblo, is a former news journalist who now practices law.

FOR FURTHER READING:

Handbook of the North American Indian, Vol. 9, Smithsonian Institution (1983)

Jewelry of the Prehistoric Southwest, E. Wesley Jernigan, School of American Research and the University of New Mexico Press (1978)

The Fetish Carvers of Zuni, Marian Rodee and James Ostler, The Maxwell Museum of Anthropology and the Pueblo of Zuni Arts and Crafts (1990)

The Turquois, Joseph E. Pogue, Memoirs of the National Academy of Sciences (1915)

Turquoise, The Gem of the Centuries, Oscar T. Branson, Treasure Chest Publications (1975)

Turquoise and the Indian, Edna Mae Bennett, Sage Books (1966)

Zuni: A Village of Silversmiths, Marian Rodee, Milford Nahohai and James Ostler, Pueblo of Zuni Arts and Crafts and The Maxwell Museum of Anthropology (1995)

Zuni Fetiches, Frank Hamilton Cushing, facsimile ed. by KC Publications (1966)

Even though Angie Reano Owen has made giant strides since fashioning plastic thunderbird necklaces to sell to servicemen, the Santo Domingo woman whose work is collected worldwide still makes it a point to also make affordable, quality pieces.

YOUNG NATIVE JEWELERS SIGNAL CHANGING OF THE GUARD

BY JON BOWMAN

Ray Tracey used to throw himself into memorizing his lines of dialogue from the television series *Hart to Hart*. Now, as one of New Mexico's pre-eminent jewelers, Tracey is more apt to ponder heartlines.

As a young man, Tracey answered Hollywood's call, leaving his home in the Navajo Nation to launch a career as an actor. He played opposite stars such as Goldie Hawn, Ricardo Montalban and Ed Asner on TV and in the movies.

He might still be acting today, except he grew weary of the parade of stereotypical Indian roles requiring him to ride around on horseback barechested. He prefers the more comfortable clothing he wears today — denim shirts, blue jeans and Nikes — although he could easily afford Armani suits with the profits from his flourishing jewelry business.

Jewelry making is just as rewarding for Angie Reano Owen, who made her first bracelets and necklaces as a child at Santo Domingo Pueblo. She remembers her parents sending her to Santa Fe to sell goods under the portal at the Palace of the Governors.

Her share of the daily proceeds amounted to less than $2, barely enough to cover the roundtrip to and from Santa Fe, and lunch at Beva's Cafe, then across from the old bus station on Water Street. If she was hungry, she ordered chile-bean soup. But if she was in the mood to splurge, she'd settle for a hamburger so she could pocket the spare change and play the jukebox.

Much has changed from the days when Owen felt lucky if she could sell a choker for $6. Now, galleries from Japan to Germany compete to showcase her work. One of her distinctive mosaic bracelets can command prices as high as $5,000.

Zuni Pueblo's Carlton Jamon also has reaped benefits from the broadening appeal of Southwest jewelry. His grandparents labored days on end to fabricate the cluster-style concho pendants popular at the time. Each teardrop-shaped turquoise stone had to be ground to perfection, and painstakingly set into place in its silver clasp.

Jamon broke from tradition, developing a novel line of fetish necklaces featuring polished and puffed silver bears soldered so perfectly the seams cannot be detected. At first, detractors lined up to attack his work. "How come you're doing this?" they admonished him. "You're not doing Zuni jewelry."

These days, Jamon spends less time deflecting critics than trying to sidetrack would-be copycats who want to know the secrets behind his methods. As his wife and partner Julie Marie confides, "If you've got a new idea, you've got to do it right away. If you don't, somebody else will, and there goes your idea."

Tracey, Owen and Jamon represent a new and innovative breed of Native American artisans. Gone are the days when jewelers only could win acceptance if they made bulky baubles — girded with massive quantities of silver and adorned with chunks of turquoise as big as horseflies.

The public's demand for elegance and openness to experimental designs motivate today's jewelers to create pieces unlike any seen before. Turquoise remains the crown jewel defining the Southwestern style, but no longer does it stand alone.

More exotic stones — the serene lapis lazuli, the regal sugilite, the iridescent opal — have expanded the rainbow of hues seen in jewelry. It's as splashy and eye-opening as the arrival of Technicolor in the movies. Sleekness and refinement are in vogue. Buyers don't measure the worth of a piece by its size so much as its inherent beauty and the integrity of its workmanship.

Tracey, Owen, Jamon and other similarly gifted talents have welcomed this shift, which has freed them to express themselves more imaginatively. They savor the opportunity to redefine the look of Southwest jewelry — to build upon the past, without slavishly following yesterday's dictates.

Here are their stories. Each is different, but taken together, they offer a composite of the changing fortunes and fashions of New Mexico's native artisans.

RAY TRACEY'S GOLDEN TOUCH

Ray Tracey is as much an ambassador as an artist. He hits the road much of the year, maintaining an itinerary of appearances that could wear a presidential hopeful down to a frazzle. Skycaps at airports from New York to Los Angeles greet him on a first-name basis. Tracey's pace is so frantic he admits he couldn't take advantage of a junket one year to Europe. Some friends drove him by the Louvre on a whirlwind tour of Paris, but the press of commitments left him no time to step inside.

He can't even sit still to design his jewelry. When he tries to do so, he draws a blank. So he keeps a pen with him at all times, knowing inspiration can strike on the freeway or the golf course as often as when he's holed up in an office.

One of his most popular abstract designs, he says, came to him while observing the patterns formed by rain whipping off the backs of semi-trucks that crowded Interstate 40 on one of his countless trips between Albuquerque and Gallup. His occasional golfing partner, retired San Francisco 49ers quarterback Steve Young, has gotten used to the sight of Tracey dawdling on a green to scribble rays, arrows and other cryptic scratches on his palm.

"I don't take credit for any of it," the self-effacing artist says. "The stuff I design does not come about through conscious thought. It's all inspiration from the environment. It's there one minute, and then it's gone."

Tracey has reason to keep up his backbreaking schedule. As the overseer of a veritable jewelry empire, Ray Tracey, Ltd., he supplies classy pieces

Right: Opting in favor of making jewelry and developing an impressive line of collector-quality pieces, Ray Tracey gave up on a promising career in the entertainment industry.

to more than 300 galleries around the world. Some 75 craftsmen, headquartered in a 4,000-square-foot warehouse in Gallup, turn out custom work to his exacting design specifications.

Besides his production shop, the entrepreneurial-minded Tracey has ventured into retailing on his own — opening a tiny shop off the Plaza in Santa Fe as well as a second outlet in Atlanta's upscale Phipps Plaza. No Native American artist since R.C. Gorman has emerged as such a marketing dynamo.

Incredibly, more than a decade ago, Tracey hadn't settled on jewelry making as his ambition in life. He was still knocking about in Hollywood, creating jewelry on the side while pursuing an acting career, most notably in the lead role of the feature film *Joe Panther*.

Hollywood held forth the opportunity for celebrity status, but jewelry making has provided him fulfillment, not to mention burgeoning fame. "I love making jewelry," he says.

Tracey's innovative designs have catapulted his jewelry above the rest. On the left is a *Yei* pendant necklace made of silver, coral, turquoise, sugilite, jet and clamshell; in the center is a silver/gold bracelet with coral and turquoise; on the right is a freshwater pearl necklace with a *Yei* pendant.

"When I've got an idea, I can't wait to get to work. It's nice to be recognized doing what I like to do."

His start as a jeweler began humbly enough. One summer, bored with nothing to do, the 9-year-old Tracey took up his mother's suggestion to attend an art class in Ganado, Ariz. She still wears the silver ring he made for her. Encouraged by Billy Malone from nearby Hubbell's Trading Post, Tracey began to mass-produce what he describes as crude belt buckles and bolo ties for pin money.

Mass production remains his forte, but sophistication is now Tracey's calling card. *Lapidary Journal* hailed his jewelry for "its clean lines and refined color." *JQ* magazine celebrated him as "a man of contrasts: seemingly low-key, yet ambitious; artistic yet businesslike; preserving traditional Native American art with a contemporary approach, and smashing stereotypes as he goes."

Tracey's signature motifs include heartline bears, stylized eagle feathers and geometric shields gracing necklaces, rings, pendants, earrings and bracelets fashioned from silver and gold. He has moved toward abstract designs and the use of exotic stones in a bid to capture broader markets.

"What we're trying to do is go really elegant — make it slick, not cluttered," he says. "High on the list is jewelry that is unusual, different and artistic. It has to be affordable — price is real important right now — but it also has to be fashionable, useful and look good."

He believes "going more mainstream" will bring greater recognition of his work as a fine art, not simply a regional craft phenomenon. "I'm getting away from the more traditional, fetish-style, Indian motifs," he says. He makes no apologies about following a tight business game plan, saying a strong marketing strategy is as crucial as artistic vision. His one regret is that all the energy he has devoted to his jewelry has made it difficult to relax with his wife Caroline and their seven children.

The physical rigors of the profession also have taken a toll. His fingerprints have disappeared from all the grinding, and he now wears glasses to do inlay work. He's even had to cut back on what used to be his greatest guilty pleasure on the road — ordering late-night, room-service banquets of chocolate cake and vanilla ice cream smothered in Hershey's syrup. "It's terrible getting old and tired," he says. "You can't see. You can't eat what you want."

PRACTICE MAKES PERFECT

Angle Reano Owen has spent the night at a bingo parlor, her way of psyching herself up to fill a massive jewelry order placed by a Japanese gallery.

"You can never work or create something when you're sad or unhappy," she says. "You have to be in the right mind, otherwise the beauty doesn't come."

Born and raised at Santo Domingo Pueblo, Owen learned to make jewelry from her parents, both skilled artisans. Too young to practice with scarce gemstones or silver, she was turned loose to assemble Thunderbird necklaces from scraps of multicolored plastic and the shells of discarded car batteries. Her mother cooked the batteries in an oven to render the material pliable.

"When the Thunderbirds became popular, we used to go down to the train station to sell them to the Army boys," she recalls.

While other kids played Hide and Seek, Owen and her sister Rose drilled heishi beads to string into necklaces. For fun, they staged contests to see who could drill the most.

"We used to envy the kids that went out dancing, that went out to the movies, because our parents were strict. We didn't do too much of that."

Owen's outgoing nature led her to become a prized sales rep for her family. She made the rounds to powwows and feast days, selling jewelry everywhere she went. She also drew an assignment to travel back and forth to Santa Fe, joining the "porch people" marketing their wares under the portal at the Palace of the Governors.

"I used to make stuff and at the same time travel to the porch," she says. "I don't recall pouting much. I was always busy."

During her youthful days on the Plaza, she occupied a spot near where her grandfather used to show his work during the Santa Fe Indian Market, when it was but a fledgling off-shoot of the annual Fiesta de Santa Fe.

Close-knit family ties heavily influenced Owen's artistic development. Her mother stressed the importance of productivity, while her father insisted on high standards.

"My father was the perfectionist," she says. "He always told us, 'Never be satisfied with what you produce. Always try to better yourself on the next piece.'"

Owen's brother Percy encouraged her to test new jewelry-making methods and materials. She remembers his attempts to develop better glues by adding chimney soot and hard residues he scraped from the chambers of wood stoves. Tourists shunned these innovations, but fellow Indian artisans, old-time traders and museum authorities began to take note of the Reanos.

It was Owen's intricate mosaic designs, however, that really turned heads. Each piece is a colorful grid, as intricate as a Cubist painting. Owen cuts hundreds, sometimes even thousands, of tiny blocks of turquoise, mother-of-pearl, jet, oyster, pipestone, coral and other materials. She glues these inlaid "chicklets" side by side on the back of a shell framework to create dazzling earrings, pendants, and bangle and cuff bracelets.

In an even more time-consuming process, she affixes the chicklet blocks to cottonwood beads that can be strung into mosaic necklaces. The chicklets are akin to sequins, except they must interlock perfectly like the pieces in a jigsaw puzzle.

Collectors from Tokyo to Milan eagerly seek out her latest offerings. She's traveled to Germany, Italy, Switzerland and France by invitation of curators who explained her work at each stop along the way. That suits her just fine. "The hardest thing to do is to talk about yourself," she says, chuckling heartily.

Owen now lives in Santa Fe, working out of a small wooden studio behind her south-side home. A dusty television broadcasts soap operas above the din of the grinders and saws

Collectors from Germany to Japan covet Angie Reano Owen's state-of-the-art jewelry. Owen credits her parents with influencing her artistic development and special attention to quality. Today, she is passing along her jewelry-making skills to her children.

that are the tools of her trade.

Like her parents, she has taken both of her own children under her wing, teaching them the intricacies of jewelry making. Her daughter Donna recently joined Montana Silversmiths as a designer. Her son Dean moonlights making belt buckles while holding down a job as a security guard.

Despite her museum-quality work, Owen isn't adverse to knocking out quick, simple, less costly pieces. "There are lots of people who can't afford the big things," she says. "It was the small things that put the bread and butter on the table years ago. I can't forget those people."

Left: Carlton and Julie Marie Jamon work in their Zuni Pueblo studio. Known for their innovative (and guardedly secret) hand-soldering techniques, the Jamons helped organize the Zuni Arts and Cultural Expo.

POWER OF THE BEAR

Nowhere do fetishes play as central a role in everyday life as at Zuni, the westernmost of New Mexico's 19 pueblos. Turtle, bear, fish and bird fetishes crowd the display cases at the Zuni Craftsman Co-op. It's not only a gallery for 450 Zuni artisans, but also the place they come to buy their supplies in bulk.

Row after row of shelves house tubs of abalone, green snail, pink mussel and cowrie shells, alongside cardboard boxes full of Sleeping Beauty turquoise. Gold and silver filaments dangle from hooks on the walls.

Carlton Jamon is among the co-op's most active members and a strong advocate for tribal arts. Along with his close friend. Tony Eriacho, he helped organize the Zuni Arts and Cultural Expo, which they hope to establish as an annual event, running simultaneously with the Inter-Tribal Indian Ceremonial in nearby Gallup.

Jamon couldn't help but notice the growing popularity of the fetishes crafted by his neighbors. His wife, Julie Marie, told him they ought to figure out a way to incorporate fetishes

Left: Boxes of raw turquoise as well as gold and silver filaments, fetishes and other raw stones await memebers of the Zuni Craftsman Co-op.

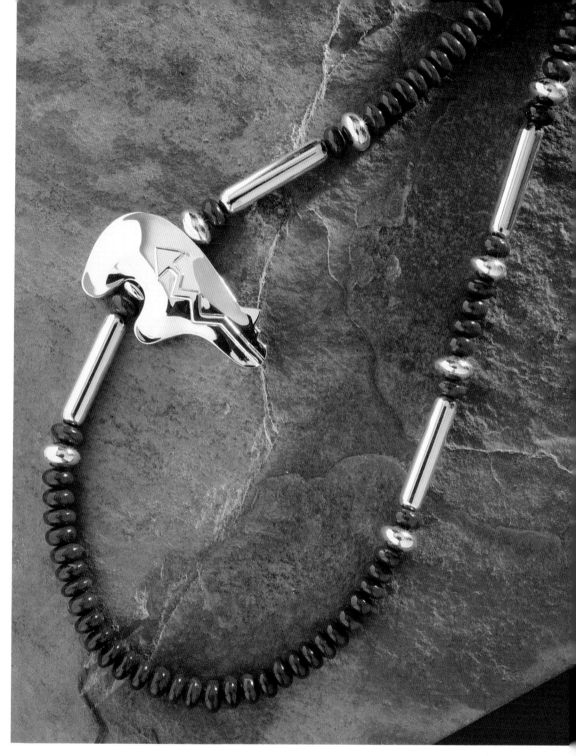

This bear fetish of sterling silver and lapis was made by Carlton and Julie Marie Jamon, both active members of the Zuni Craftsman Co-op.

Left: Tony Eriacho and wife, Ola, prefer traditional motifs to the new designs sprouting up every day.

into their own work. But as a jeweler, Jamon didn't know what to make of the carvings.

The solution, he says, came to him almost magically as he slept. "I had a dream about it," he recalls. "I dreamed I was doing it and then when I woke up, I made it. Everything fell into place perfectly. I didn't have to reject any stones. Everything was just right."

His creation: a bear fetish necklace, composed of hollow sterling silver talismans strung on strands of black onyx, turquoise, pearls, heishi and coral. Jamon's hand-soldering techniques gave these bears a sleek, streamlined appearance, transforming a traditional symbol of power and strength into something as light, gossamer-smooth and beautiful as a butterfly.

Although certain purists cried foul, collectors have embraced the new design. Demand has grown so great that Julie Marie, a Navajo raised in Toadlena, now spends much of her time helping her husband craft jewelry, rather than weaving the Two Grey Hills-style tapestries that once earned her wide acclaim.

Jamon learned the basics of soldering from his grandmother when he was 14, but he didn't get serious about jewelry making until he had finished college and tried a few other professions.

In that regard, he is similar to his friend Eriacho, who worked in construction and uranium mining before turning to creating jewelry with his wife Ola. (Yes, she says, she does "get razzed a lot" about her name, evoking Zuni's famed Olla maidens known for their capacity to carry large pots on their heads.)

Although both couples hail from Zuni, they didn't know each other until they met at an art show in Denver. Now, they are each other's most ardent supporters, an ironic twist in as

Tony and Ola Eriacho of Zuni pueblo created these intricately designed bracelets with mother-of-pearl, gold, Acoma jet and Sleeping Beauty turquoise.

much as their styles are poles apart.

Ola Eriacho proudly proclaims she "is sticking with the traditional," using turquoise instead of any of the newer stones. She favors geometric, sun-face designs because they reflect her heritage as a member of Zuni's Sun Clan.

The Eriachos also report brisk sales, except during the 1993 hantavirus scare when tourists deserted the region en masse. "We had to produce a lot of little things, we had to scale down then," Ola says. "The hantavirus, that hurt everybody."

In today's eclectic jewelry market, there's a place for the trailblazers, as well as those who uphold time-honored traditions.

Jon Bowman is the associate publisher of *New Mexico Magazine*. He writes free-lance for a variety of publications, specializing in motion pictures.

Treated or untreated? The top three rows show natural low-grade turquoise (left) and turquoise treated with oils, waxes and plastics (right). Note the dish of crushed "chalk" turquoise with a piece of reconstituted turquoise on the lower right. Reconstituted turquoise is made by mixing the "chalk" with plastic and pressing in into block molds. The cross on the lower left is stabilized with plastic.

BUYER BEWARE:
HIDDEN FACETS OF TURQUOISE

BY RICHARD McCORD

Just as all that glitters is not gold, not every lovely looking gemstone that beckons you with mystical aquamarine allure is true-blue turquoise. Not by a long shot.

"Only 10 percent of the turquoise being mined today is gem grade," says Joe Lowry Sr., proprietor of the Turquoise Museum in Albuquerque and an authority on the subject. Therefore, a full nine-tenths of the turquoise going into jewelry and pottery has been altered in one way or another.

And when outright fake turquoise, which is nothing but colored plastic, is factored into the equation, only the tiniest fraction of what is presented as "turquoise" in the marketplace is the genuine, natural, untreated real thing.

Not all of this is bad, however. There is a proper place for every form of turquoise and turquoise-seeming substance — as long as it is openly and honestly represented. Moreover, the sharply lower prices of the altered stones can make handsome turquoise items accessible to countless buyers who could never afford the cost of a natural gem.

The price differential is indeed significant. Highest-quality natural gems, already cut and polished, might sell for more than $1,500 per pound in a jewelers' supply store (in this form, however, they usually are sold by the carat). Even in the rough, encased in impure rock that must be chipped and ground away, gem-grade natural turquoise can cost $350 a pound or more. By contrast, lower-grade stones that have been "stabilized" might bring from $40 to $250 per pound. And a pound of manufactured plastic, sold in chunks called "block turquoise," can go for as little as $10.

The problem is many unscrupulous vendors sell altered or fake products to gullible first-time buyers at inflated prices, promising all the while that, "Yes, ma'am, this is genuine, gem-grade, all-natural turquoise."

According to museum-director Lowry, the ranking of turquoise, from the highest to the lowest, goes like this:

• Large natural gems — The most highly valued turquoise pieces are large, bright blue stones, formed hard enough by nature to hold their shine and color all through the years.

Because each stone is different, cost might be affected by the matrix pattern, the name of the mine, the beauty in the eye of the beholder and other factors. Such gems are quite rare, however, and few artists can find or afford them.

• Lesser natural gems with good blue or green color — Though not big enough for, say, bolo ties or concho belts, these pieces are fine for rings or inlaid jewelry. They come in varying degrees of hardness, however, and all but the hardest might over the course of time absorb oil, which changes the stone's color. Therefore, items made with such stones must be kept away from dishwater, hand lotion, baby oil or anything else that might get into the turquoise.

• Stabilized — Beginning in the 1960s, highly technical processes were devised for "stabilizing" low-grade natural turquoise, called "chalk" in the industry, because often it is almost white in color and is quite soft. When these stones are treated under high pressure with a clear plastic resin, they absorb the solution and emerge as bright blue or green stones almost indistinguishable from high-quality natural gems. This is a permanent treatment, thus the turquoise never fades and is impervious to oils and other liquids. Though not as prized as natural gems, stabilized is considered a fully legitimate form of turquoise — as long as the alteration is acknowledged. Many of the finest turquoise artists, Indian and non-Indian, work with it to make beautiful items that sell at non-collector prices.

• Dyed stabilized — Although clear plastic brings out a stone's "natural" color when absorbed, some stabilizers add dyes to the solution to create a deeper, darker blue. Most dealers and artists do not care for dyed gems, which have an artificial look. But some buyers prefer these colors, and so turquoise altered in this way continues to be produced.

• Reconstituted — Whereas stabilizing permanently hardens large pieces, the "reconstituting" process begins with tiny chips of turquoise, mixes them with epoxy, then treats them under pressure to create nicely colored chunks big enough to make into jewelry. Although a permanently treated form of turquoise, reconstituted is lesser in rank than stabilized.

• Temporarily treated — There are myriad ways to enhance the look of low-quality turquoise temporarily, and numerous shady characters are eager to do so long enough to make a sale. Anything that turquoise absorbs can deepen its color: oil, paraffin, lacquer, polishes, powders, pulverized abrasives, silicon carbide, aluminum oxide, even water. Methods for applying these agents include rubbing, soaking, tumbling, boiling on the kitchen stove or baking in the oven. The durability of these treatments varies, from days to months. But eventually the deep color will fade, leaving a bleached and unattractive stone that once gleamed bright.

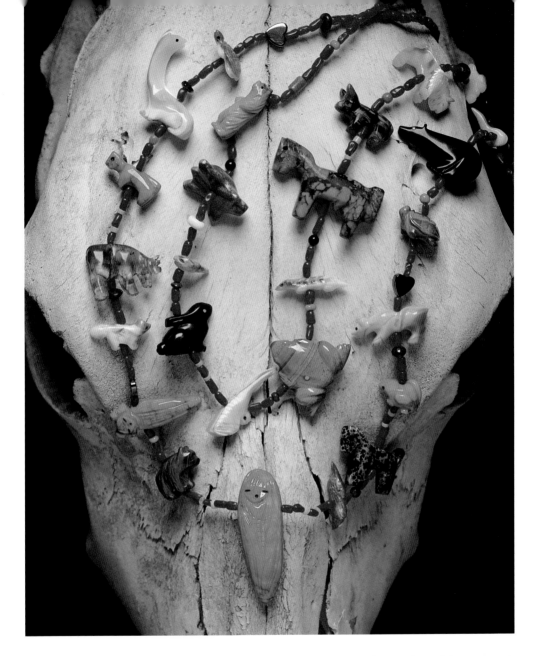

This Zuni "Grandmother's" necklace of various animal fetishes was made by members of the renowned Quandelacy family, including Steward, Faye, Ellen, Georgia, Andres, Barlow and Sandra as well as Alenita and Bryan Yunie. (Necklace courtesy of Keshi, the Zuni Connection, Santa Fe)

Two beautiful turquoise stones are surrounded by natural "rough" chalk turquoise. The two stabilized stones originally were "chalk," but they were treated under high pressure with a clear plastic resin that brought out the brighter shades.

• Imitation — The bottom rung of the turquoise ladder is held by material that is not turquoise at all, but plastic imitations of it. Although colors and even matrix patterns can be approximated, plastic turquoise can melt, scratch, lose luster, fade and generally cease to be attractive not long after it is bought. But there are tons of it on the market, and too-trusting buyers are frequently fooled.

To further complicate the picture, plastic turquoise is often used in machine-stamped silver jewelry manufactured in places like Taiwan or Korea, or made in New Mexico by non-Indian workers, and then sold as handmade Native American.

The buying public has heard about this vast influx of fake or altered turquoise, but the subject is too complex to be readily understood. Consequently, recent years have seen a growing apprehension in the marketplace.

"There is a knock-off factor in every aspect of Indian art," says Santa Fe dealer Bill

Hawn, noting that shoppers were less wary a decade ago. "If there were no pitfalls, the business would still be very strong. But there are pitfalls, and fake turquoise is one."

And today's buyer needs to be wary to avoid getting taken. Generally speaking, street vendors and truck stops are more likely to misrepresent their turquoise than are established stores in tourist centers like Santa Fe and Albuquerque. But deception is where you find it.

Investigative reports by television stations in Albuquerque found altered and phony turquoise being sold as natural stone by Native American vendors, by clerks in shops, even by owners of well-known trading posts. The reports stressed that such practices are violations of both state and federal laws. But even after the exposé, the responsible authorities "did nothing — nothing" to crack down on misrepresentations, reported investigative reporter Larry Barker.

Barker conducted an investigative report in 2004 that uncovered many instances of fake turquoise by Native American vendors in downtown Santa Fe. The report prompted the proprietors of the La Fonda to ban all vendors from selling their wares on the perimeter sidewalks of the hotel, ending a decades-long tradition.

The primary reason more is not done is a simple lack of manpower, responded Roberta

Blocks of plastic can be made to look strikingly similar to real turquoise, sometimes requiring an expert to tell the difference and often fooling unsuspecting buyers.

Joe, who worked as an assistant attorney general in New Mexico's Consumer Protection Division in the 1990s.

"Our entire division (had) only one investigator," she sighed. "With these limitations, it is difficult to go out and drum up cases. So we take them one at a time, usually after a complaint. In most cases, however, we do succeed in getting a voluntary refund when a complaint is made."

Ultimately, then, the best safeguard against getting taken in the turquoise game is

Left: The charm of Native-made turquoise jewelry continues to enthrall tourists such as this woman perusing pieces under the portal of the Palace of the Governors in Santa Fe.

the oldest rule of all: *caveat emptor*. "In this business it's be wise or beware," says Bob Ward, a longtime Indian art dealer in Santa Fe.

Even a little knowledge goes a long way in avoiding the most common pitfalls. And it can be quick and cheap to acquire. Albuquerque's Turquoise Museum offers daily half-hour seminars, at a nominal cost, to teach consumers how to proceed with confidence.

The cheapest plastic turquoise is easily spotted, museum director Lowry says, because it simply does not look real. Most temporarily treated stones are also detectable, because they have an oily look. For higher-cost pieces that are not openly identified as stabilized, he recommends getting an expert opinion, even if only from another shopkeeper. In nine out of 10 cases, he says, only an expert can spot the altered pieces.

The mere appearance of knowledge on the part of the consumer is a powerful tool itself. When questions are asked about a stone's authenticity, unscrupulous sellers know that false answers can leave them open to fines and prosecution, and so they are more likely to reply honestly.

Somewhat ironically, an item's price is in most cases a fairly good indicator of the value of the material in it. Earrings selling for $6 or bracelets going for $10 cannot possibly be of high-quality turquoise, no matter what the vendor claims. And for any item over $35, Lowry insists, the buyer should ask for a written description of the gem's quality, as required by New Mexico law. A seller refusing this request should not be dealt with at all.

In the end, however, the surest way to know exactly what grade of turquoise you're getting is to deal with shops and artists of high reputation and institutions of unquestioned integrity, such as Santa Fe's Indian Market.

Whether your budget is $5 or $5,000, whether you demand natural gems of rarest quality or would happily settle for nicely treated stones at one-sixth the cost, whether you seek a stunning heirloom or a cheap memento, the perfect piece of alluring blue substance — natural, altered or faux — is just waiting for you. But as you go looking, never forget that it's a jungle out there: A turquoise jungle.

In addition to the sources cited in the article above, the writer wishes to acknowledge the assistance of others who provided information that was invaluable and greatly appreciated. They are: Cornelis "Kase" Klein, professor, Department of Earth and Planetary Sciences, University of New Mexico; appraiser and broker Joan Caballero, former president, Southwestern Association of Indian Arts; and turquoise stabilizer Gary Werner, head of Gary Werner Mining and Processing Co., Albuquerque.

Richard McCord is a free-lance writer and columnist, and former New York City journalist who in 1974 founded the weekly *Santa Fe Reporter.*

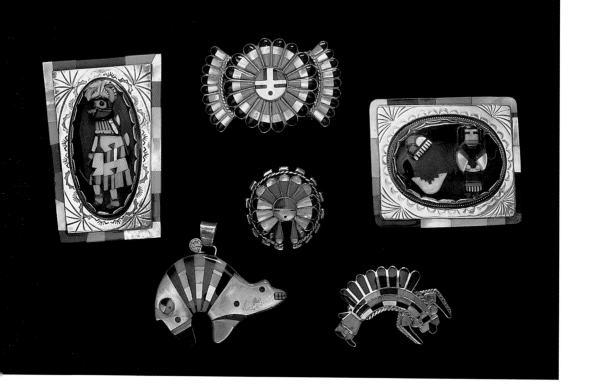

Above: The only piece that is Zuni-made in this grouping is the bolo tie clip by Ronnie Calavaza on the left, while all the other pieces are made in the Philippines. Many Native artists concede that foreign copies can be hard to tell from Native originals, especially when unscrupulous dealers remove the required import stickers. Dealing directly with the artist or reputable dealers is the only way buyers can be sure their purchase is native made and incorporates high-quality stones and silver.

Below: The piece on the left, *Rainbow Man*, is by Zuni artist Fadrian Bowannie, the piece on the right is a copy form the Philippines.

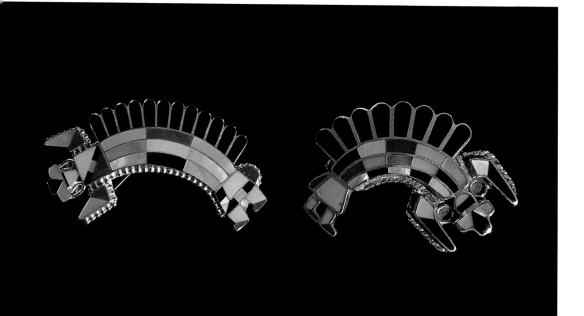

COPYCATS
FLOOD THE MARKET

BY GAYE BROWN DE ALVAREZ, PHOTOGRAPHY BY STEVE LARESE

Zuni jewelers Tony and Ola Eriacho were thrilled when *New Mexico Magazine* featured several of their hand-made pieces of jewelry in the first edition of *The Allure of Turquoise*, and then again when author Theda Bassman chose their work for her book *Treasures of the Zuni*.

Jewelers for more than 20 years, the couple had a large customer base in the Midwest, the East Coast and overseas and were making a good living.

Then one day they were at the Phoenix Flea Market and they noticed some jewelry that looked similar to their pieces in the two books. On closer inspection, the flea market jewelry was exactly like their one-of-a-kind pieces, except for the hallmark stamped on the back. "These pieces were made overseas and the stickers (indicating point of origin) were removed," Eriacho says. "There was just a 'sterling' stamp on the back."

More and more, they began seeing "knockoffs" of their work and hearing more complaints from Zuni artists that the intricate jewelry, made in the style distinctive to the state's largest pueblo, 35 miles south of Gallup, was being made overseas and shipped to the U.S. and sold as Native American handmade.

Every year, attendance at both the Gallup Inter-Tribal Indian Ceremonial and the Santa Fe Indian Market reaches record numbers. Many of those tourists and sightseers will buy what New Mexico and the Southwest is famous for — Indian art and Indian jewelry.

But buyer beware! Like many collectibles, the market is flooded with cheap imitations and even impressive look-alikes from sweatshops in the Philippines, Taiwan and other areas where labor is cheap. There are ways to assure that the item purchased is genuine and Indian hand-made, not a knockoff from the other side of the globe.

Indian art is protected under the Indian Arts and Crafts Act of 1990. The act prohibits misrepresentation in marketing of Indian arts and crafts products within the U.S., stating in essence, that it is illegal to offer or display for sale, or sell any art or craft product in a manner that falsely suggests it is Indian produced, an Indian product, or the product of an Indian tribe.

Turquoise and Navajo weaving expert Joe Tanner of Gallup welcomed the opportunity

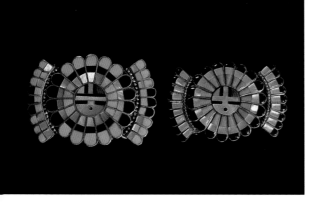

to discuss how to purchase an original piece of Indian art. A ceremonial judge and a fourth-generation turquoise dealer and Indian trader who lives and works in Gallup, Tanner just returned from Hong Kong and mainland China, where, he says, much of the world's turquoise processing currently takes place.

"After a trip like I've just come from, you're very aware of what a wonderful collectible commodity is being sold in New Mexico," Tanner says. "One-of-a-kinds are rare and what we have in this state are artisans doing what they want, where they want and when they want, to create a one-of-a-kind piece. It's a rare thing. Wearable art."

Tanner says that for each 100 pounds of ore taken from a turquoise mine, only 3-10 pounds is natural and of gem quality. The rest has to be strengthened or altered in some way to make it saleable.

Above: The pin on the left by J.D. Massie is real, while the one on the right a copy made in the Philippines.

Below: The bolo tie clip on the left by Ronnie Calavaza is real; the one on the right is a copy made in the Philippines.

"However, that three to 10 pounds," Tanner says, "is so hard to find, so fulfilling, is so worth the chase. Like the diamond."

Is there an easy way to test turquoise to see if it is natural or treated?

"No," Tanner says. Not to the novice eye. There are some old wives' tales, for example,

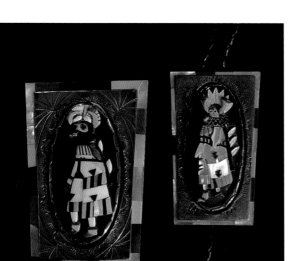

if you heat a wood-burning tool and touch it to the turquoise, and it melts, you're not dealing with a stone. Another so-called test is to run a hot pin over the surface, and if it leaves a mark, it's not natural turquoise. While these may be good tests for plastic, not all turquoise treatment processes involve plastic.

"Turquoise hard chalk impregnated with resin looks and acts like turquoise," Tanner explained. Another "test" is to take a

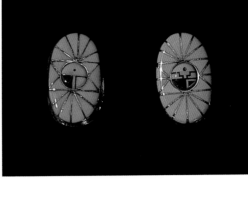

pocketknife, and if you cannot scratch the surface, the turquoise must be rock. Not perfect, Tanner says.

There is only one way to assure the purchased piece is of collectible quality, hand-made by a Native American artisan, Tanner says. It is a learning process in itself. Read books, visit museums and galleries and take note of the pieces on display, visit trading posts, the Inter-Tribal Ceremonial in Gallup and the Indian Market in Santa Fe and meet the artists personally. Get acquainted with collectible pieces; compare them with flea market pieces. Depend on a truthful seller. And regardless of whom you buy from, demand an invoice that identifies, in writing, the source of the stone, whether or not it is natural or treated, whether the metalsmithing is hand done or spin cast and have the seller sign the invoice.

"Once you've seen the best, it takes a high quality to please you," Tanner says, and added, "it is so worth the chase."

Above: The ring on the right is by Ola Eriacho, the other is a copy.

Below: The belt buckle on top is by Zuni artists Leander and Lisa Othole, and the other is a copy from the Philippines

As for Navajo rugs, Tanner says, "once you choose the perfect Navajo weaving for your environment there is no other art in the world that can replace it."

With Navajo weavings, it is easier to spot imitations, he says. "Weavings from Mexico and other parts of the world exploit Navajo patterns, but they aren't Navajo and not necessarily handmade.

"I associate the word 'tapestry' with quality," he says. "A fine tapestry weave usually means 60 wefts (the vertical part of the weave) per inch." The rule for the designs, dyes and colors in the rug are simple, and the color mix and design should please you, Tanner says.

"Navajo weaving is some of the great art of the world," Tanner says. "I never consider a sale final until they enjoy that piece for 24 hours. If the bells

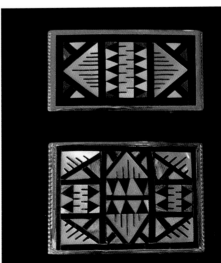

ring, keep it."

Tanner admits that buying rugs on the street in Gallup is a safer bet than jewelry but then again, "back to that invoice."

Collector and historian Martin Link of Gallup has devoted much of his time lately to preserving the integrity of Native American arts and crafts. Co-owner and publisher of *The Indian Trader* for more than 15 years and former museum director for the Navajo tribe, Link knows the difficulty in differentiating foreign-made items from the genuine thing.

"You can't tell," he says, elaborating that there is no simple way to test a piece for authenticity.

He told the story of a company that after seeing the beautiful Hopi overlay pieces in

Left: The book featuring Tony and Ola Eriacho's work, together with the pieces made in the Philippines that are almost exact copies of their designs offer an eye-opening comparison.

Theda Bassman's book, *The Beauty of Hopi Jewelry*, they set up shop in Thailand and started reproducing all the items in the book with sterling silver. They pilfered Zuni and Navajo styles and sold them over the Internet for $1 a gram. His Website (www.buckagram.com) states that the items for sale are made in Asia and explains how most pieces on the market now are not made by Native Americans. Further, "scams like this have been going on for many, many years so please do not point the finger at me for anything."

The jewelry is then sent to market, Link explained, with a sticker on the back indicating the piece was "Made in Thailand." But, Link says, once the sticker is peeled off, it is next to impossible to differentiate the piece from genuine Hopi, Zuni or Navajo handmade.

Link says that it hardly matters to people looking to pick up $5 souvenirs from Indian Country, but for those seeking collectibles, the only way to be certain of authenticity is to deal with a reputable trader or artist, and always get a receipt.

"There are no really great deals on Indian jewelry," Link says. "A $5 bolo tie is just a $5 bolo tie."

There are large supply houses in Gallup that sell anything and everything to handcraft jewelry. From sheets of gold and silver, and huge rocks of the best turquoise available in the world to machine-made beads and plastic malachite, the supply houses are truthful about what they sell and can offer education on the millions of different items for sale.

A person can walk into Thunderbird Supply on West 66 or Indian Jeweler's Supply on Coal Avenue and buy eight silver conchos and a matching silver belt buckle. All that is needed is a piece of leather to string the items together, and they have a genuine concho belt. It takes an expert to tell that the conchos are machine-made or spin cast and not handmade. At these supply houses, items such as rings with shanks, bezels and silver ornamentation can be bought — the buyer selects the stones (treated or natural) to go in the bezels — already precut to the perfect size, and *voila!* A Southwestern ring.

But no Native American ever touched the silver or the stones — they were machine manufactured. Unless, of course, a Native American buys the prefab pieces, assembles them and sells them, which is common in the Gallup area.

"This is the difference between handmade and handcrafted," says Tony Eriacho, who is part of a crusade to educate the public on the dangers facing the industry of Indian arts and crafts. He travels around the Southwest, setting up displays with fine Zuni jewelry next to identical pieces, made in Taiwan or the Philippines. He defies anyone to tell the difference. Most people can't.

A group of Native Americans, hoping to foster, develop and contribute to the support and understanding of authentic Indian arts and crafts started the Council for Indigenous Arts and Culture (CIAC), a nonprofit organization providing education and working with law enforcement to preserve the integrity of native handmade arts and crafts. They are currently soliciting members and funds, and have published a list of businesses that sell Indian art with a commitment to authenticity and honest representation. They are looking to expand the list.

CIAC will set up displays at nine visitors' centers along New Mexico highways to educate travelers to seek authentic Indian handmade arts and crafts, and they offer education to groups that ask. They are committed to protecting the livelihood of their fellow Indian artists.

Yes, it's hard to tell the difference between Indian handmade and an overseas knockoff. But the one thing that all the experts agree on?

Always, get a receipt.

Gaye Brown de Alvarez is the features editor for the *Gallup Independent* and has written a memoirs/cookbook and a novel about northern Mexico and the drug trade.

TIPS ON FINDING AUTHENTIC PIECES

JEWELRY

• Nickel silver can be differentiated from sterling silver with hydrochloric acid. If it turns green where the acid has touched the silver, it indicates copper content and is considered "nickel" or "German" silver.*

• Look for "hallmarks" or artist's stamps on the back of the piece.**

• Educate yourself. Look at pieces in museums and high-end reputable stores. Meet the artists. Deal with reputable sellers.

• If purchasing a piece, insist on an invoice stating the source of the stone, whether it is treated or not; the artist's name and tribal affiliation; whether the metalsmithing is done by hand or spin cast; whether it is handmade or handcrafted and have the seller sign the invoice.

* This is only an indication of silver quality. Many Plains tribes artists fashion jewelry from German silver.

** Artists stamps are also being duplicated and used by non-native artisans to fool buyers into thinking the piece was Indian handmade.

POTTERY

• Indian handmade pottery is never made on a wheel. It is built up with coils of clay that are then smoothed over.

- Indian pottery does not have a flat base or look like it was "cut" off a pottery wheel.
- Look for artist's name and/or tribal affiliation on the bottom of the pot.
- Indian handmade pottery is not glazed. Some pottery has a shiny finish that is the result of polishing, not glossy commercial glazes.

RUGS
- Rugs should have straight edges and no rolled up corners.
- A tapestry-quality rug usually means 60 wefts per inch. (A saddle blanket has a coarser weave).
- Deal with a reputable seller and get an invoice. Many world weavers exploit Navajo and other native patterns so it is very difficult to differentiate between native and non-native made.

NEED MORE INFORMATION?
Council for Indigenous Arts and Culture
Western Office
P.O. Box 912
Zuni, N.M. 87327
(505) 869-8148
www.ciaccouncil.org

Indian Arts and Crafts Board
U.S. Department of the Interior
1849 C Street NW
MS4004-MIB
Washington, DC 20240

Southwest Association for Indian Arts Inc.
P.O. Box 969
Santa Fe, N.M. 87504
(505) 983-5220
www.swaia.org

This Navajo couple enjoys a measure of prosperity thanks to the husband's ability as a silversmith. They live on the world's largest reservation whose people are well known for their beautiful rugs and jewelry. (*New Mexico Magazine* Archival Collection, photographer unknown)

THE PLIGHT
OF OLD PAWN

BY JACK HARTSFIELD

The saga of old pawn takes on all the elements of a Tony Hillerman mystery, complete with folklore, deception and ceremonial rituals in the midst of a vanishing era in New Mexico.

To Southwest Indians, silver and turquoise jewelry always ranked as the finest form of personal adornment, but by the turn of the century, it also became an asset with a known value that could be pawned at outlying trading posts for credit and everyday necessities. The term old pawn emerges from those early transactions and refers to the turquoise and silver pieces, originally intended for personal use, that were pawned between 1890 and 1940.

Trading posts began springing up as early as the 1870s in the fledgling Territory of New Mexico. The Santo Domingo Indian Trading Post opened in 1881 on the fringe of the pueblo south of Santa Fe where the Atchison, Topeka & Santa Fe Railway established a rail center. There, jewelry could be traded for a partial sum of its worth in cash or goods.

If the pawn was not redeemed and interest paid within a given time, it was declared "dead." The trader could then name his price and sell it. Even so, many Southwestern traders were reluctant to sell the pawn right away, since they understood the importance of the silver and turquoise ornaments as signs of status and wealth.

The whereabouts of much old pawn is a mystery today, but the stones reputedly came from the once prolific Cerrillos (Chalchihuitl, Tiffany and Castillian) mines near Santa Fe, in the nation's oldest mining district. Santo Domingo Pueblo had historically laid claim to the dormant volcanic cone where the preferred azure blue turquoise could be found close to the surface. They revered the stones as personal ornaments to ward off misfortune and disease.

In 1890 a Zuni trader, Kineshde, is said to have negotiated an arrangement with Santo Domingo to mount Cerrillos turquoise on Zuni silver pieces. Zuni craftsmen learned the art of silversmithing around 1860 from the Spanish.

By the 1920s, silver and turquoise jewelry from New Mexico had become a highly valued commodity, an art form that intrigued buyers from the East Coast aboard the Atchison, Topeka & Santa Fe Railway. The buyers quickly learned they could demand high dollars from

collectors across the United States and Europe. High-quality turquoise from Cerrillos could bring as much as $25 a carat, 140 carats to the ounce, about 100 times more expensive per ounce than gold in 1907.

Prices today fluctuate, governed mostly by how much a buyer is willing to pay, but the lure to own authentic old pawn or antique Indian jewelry is as strong as ever. This jewelry has virtually disappeared from the open market and is difficult to find. Private collectors and museums hold much of it, some privately hoarded as far away as the Middle East. Dealers in Santa Fe, Albuquerque, Gallup, Taos and Farmington still offer antique silver and turquoise ornaments, maybe old pawn and maybe not, but they, too, admit an era is close to the end.

"Much of what some call old pawn today is a misnomer," says Robert Ashton, an anthropologist and former buyer in Santa Fe. "I prefer to call it antique jewelry." In the 1990s Ashton displayed a treasure trove of silver and turquoise ornaments at a Santa Fe gallery on historic Canyon Road, much of it including ingot or coin silverwork before 1930 with hand-cut natural turquoise stones.

The late Shah of Iran, for instance, once held what might have been New Mexico old pawn turquoise and silver in his private collection — fooled by sellers who passed it off as antique, high-quality Persian turquoise.

The cuts of the stones, the silverwork and craftsmanship involved can usually authenticate whether it is older jewelry, says Ashton, but establishing its authenticity can seldom be clearly defined beyond any doubt. Without a clear-cut, documented chain of possession from the time of creation through a string of owners to the last owner, there can only be educated guesses.

Gallup, situated along New Mexico's western border at the doorsteps of the sprawling Navajo Reservation, long has been considered the commercial source of 80 percent of the nation's marketable high-quality Indian jewelry. But even in Gallup, little if any antique jewelry sells on the open market. A new, thriving contemporary silver and turquoise jewelry market in Gallup is partially controlled by Palestinian merchants, who have formed a working relationship with the Zuni.

The Palestinians, first represented by the arrival of Jim Rashid who started selling rugs from the trunk of his car then Zuni jewelry, aren't reputed to be collectors of antique jewelry, but as sellers of silver and turquoise ornaments manufactured in the last few decades.

"What we're after is silver and turquoise jewelry made before World War II," Ashton says. "I could spend a month in Gallup and maybe, just maybe, I could come up with three or four questionable pieces on the open market that may fall in that category."

Such personal jewelry was not crafted for commercial sale. Rather, Native Americans

Opposite: A Navajo silversmith forges jewelry in his hogan sometime in the late 1930s. A piece of railroad iron shown in the foreground is his anvil. (*New Mexico Magazine* Archival Collection, photographer unknown)

Right: These old pawn Navajo bracelets were made of coin silver before 1920. The third bracelet from the right is set with Hubbell glass beads. (Bracelets courtesy of Morning Star Gallery, Santa Fe)

Here are several aged Zuni inlay pins (circa 1930-1940) set with turquoise, spiny oyster, mother-of-pearl and jet. (Jewelry courtesy of Morning Star Gallery, Santa Fe)

quickly used it as an alternative to pawn when many tourists and buyers came to the West earlier this century, he says.

"There was a time when I'd stuff my boots with cash and head to the pawn rooms and come back with exquisite silver and turquoise jewelry spread out on my bed," says one veteran buyer who spent decades browsing through racks in Gallup and Farmington.

"As late as the 1970s, there was great availability of antique silver and turquoise, or old pawn, but not any more," she says. "It's not there."

Today, collectors pay healthy prices for the privilege of ownership, ranging from less than $500 for a single piece to thousands of dollars for others deemed to be the best in craftsmanship and design.

The most prized include Pueblo pins, Zuni Butterfly pins, Zuni Antelope Kachina pins, concho belts, Navajo bracelets with turquoise inlays, ketohs (bow guards), Navajo jacia (ear strings) and turquoise bead necklaces, and ornate squash blossom necklaces.

The late Virginia Doneghy of Minneapolis, Minn., established a private collection of authentic antique silver and turquoise jewelry, much of it designated as old pawn, from New Mexico. She spent more than 20 years, between 1940 and 1960, amassing her private collection.

When Doneghy died in 1982 she willed her collection to the Minneapolis Institute of the Arts, which several years ago auctioned off portions to the highest bidders. Morning Star Gallery in Santa Fe wound up with some of Doneghy's treasures.

Some pawn jewelry could easily have been crafted since the 1960s, a result of Indian craftsmen latching on to the concept of fashioning silver and turquoise jewelry specifically for commercial intent, then pawning it with no intention whatsoever of retrieving it from the pawn racks.

Ellis Tanner, a fourth-generation trader in the Gallup area and owner of Ellis Tanner Trading Co., says bluntly about old pawn, "There isn't any." The soaring demand over what once was an abundant supply led many Native Americans with heirloom pieces to sell out to the highest bidders. Tanner, whose great grandfather came to the area as a trader in 1870, says there is jewelry made to appear antique or old pawn.

"Some of the work is pretty good," he says. "There isn't really anything wrong with that as long as it isn't represented to be something it isn't. The secret for buyers is to make certain they are dealing with a reputable dealer."

A reputable dealer who has been in the business long enough to do his or her homework develops a sixth sense about the likely age of a piece by carefully examining the stones and silverwork involved, and by determining if and how the stones were chemically treated.

Expert appraisers say they can more easily identify the work of a particular silversmith than determine a specific decade in which the jewelry was made. Even then, an experienced buyer or dealer can be fooled — but not often.

"Anybody who says they can't be fooled, is a fool," Ashton says. "I've been had a few times, only to discover later that I overlooked something in the piece that should have told me I knew better."

The watchdog agency trying to keep the silver and turquoise industry honest is the Albuquerque-based Indian Arts and Crafts Association, with more than 600 members nationwide, including traders, museums, collectors, individual Indian craftspeople, tribal co-ops and guilds.

The association has developed a worldwide security system to maintain high ethical standards and reduce the theft of Indian arts. IACA has the power to eject any of its members when misrepresentations are made about any item up for sale and to turn over information to authorities if there are possible violations of federal, state or local law. The program is proving effective, but faces some challenges.

Even pawn or old pawn, positively identified, isn't necessarily more valuable than recently made contemporary silver and turquoise jewelry — unless exquisite craftsmanship is obvious.

John Kania of Santa Fe's Kania-Ferrin Gallery says it's been years since he's had a piece of silver and turquoise jewelry complete with a pawn ticket. "Even if it has an old tag, who cares?" he says. "If the tag could be verified as pre-World War II, it might or might not mean something. . . ."

Kania appraises his cache of silver and turquoise ornaments by determining whether the silver was hand-pounded, chiseled or filed, whether it is ingot or coin silver or whether the silversmith signed or stamped his work, a practice that began about 1950 for jewelry specifically manufactured for commercial sale.

The quality of silver used in a piece of jewelry also hints of the region where it was produced. Plains Indian silversmiths, for instance, often used what is called German silver, which isn't silver at all, but an alloy of copper, zinc and nickel. Indian silversmiths in the Southwest use sterling silver, which is 925 parts silver and 75 parts copper as set by law.

A good quality piece of antique jewelry would be something dated prior to 1940, Kania says, but even that wouldn't necessarily mean it was Indian-made for personal use. It might well be a commercial ornament crafted for tourist jewelry, sometimes called Fred Harvey jewelry, sold to early train travelers heading West.

Sometimes a remarkable event can change history and perceptions in the business. Many dealers and buyers in the silver and turquoise trade believed the last vestiges of Cerrillos turquoise had been mined near Santa Fe in 1947 by a team hired by the Girard family of Butte, Mont., forerunners of Anaconda Mining. Turquoise had been mined at Tyrone and at Santa Rita and Hachita in southern New Mexico, but none was as fine as that coming from Cerrillos.

If, for instance, Cerrillos turquoise was depleted, then whatever silver and turquoise jewelry could be tied to Cerrillos had to have been made at the latest in 1947, if not much earlier. That, say gemologists and lapidarists, could enhance the value of such jewelry as antique if not old pawn.

In March 1983, through a series of blunders, the then New Mexico State Highway Department hauled off mine tailings on Turquoise Hill at Cerrillos near Santa Fe to be used as a road base for N.M. 22, now N.M. 586. Twenty-eight thousand tons of tailings were spread out in a dusty row 8 feet wide, 4 feet high and seven miles long along the roadway. A weekend snow exposed raw turquoise gemstones and artifacts. More than 400 amateur collectors clamored to pick up the turquoise, stone hammers and other artifacts from the tailings.

These three early Navajo pieces are from left: a second-phase concho belt made from coin silver, circa 1890; a second-phase concho belt with a pictorial buckle made of coin silver, circa 1910; and a first-phase "open center" concho belt made of coin silver, circa 1875-1885. (Jewelry courtesy of Morning Star Gallery, Santa Fe)

Then Gov. Toney Anaya ordered all 28,000 tons hauled back to the mine property on March 28,1983, in a futile attempt to undo what had been done. The best estimates were that it cost $360,000 to return the tailings to the property. It was an eye-opener, however, that Cerrillos turquoise still existed, some likely passed off as the last of the gemstones from Turquoise Hill, perhaps fashioned into jewelry "antiquities."

Cheryl Ingram, co-owner of Silver Sun in Santa Fe, says she initially doubted the stories that followed — some said there was at least $2 million worth of turquoise in the tailings — until she bought polished turquoise from a custodian assigned to the property after the debacle. She was told that as many as 75 different hues, matrixes and colors of turquoise were discovered in the tailings, more variations than experts had ever identified at any single mine.

Ingram brought out displays of polished Cerrillos turquoise, all gleaned from tailings in the late 1980s and some in the '90s, awaiting the right craftsman to fashion it into contemporary silver and turquoise ornaments. The Cerrillos mine property today is fenced, under lock and key, and posted no trespassing.

The most heralded product to come from the Cerrillos mine is the renowned 3-pound silver and turquoise squash blossom necklace on display at the Millicent Rogers Museum in Taos. The necklace once appraised at $500,000, but its worth today is unknown and it is not for sale. Zuni silversmith Keekyadeyuse fashioned the necklace, using Cerrillos turquoise around 1945 — meaning even the most famous piece was not old pawn and was first made for commercial sale, says Guadalupe Tafoya, a director of the Taos museum.

Presumably much of the true old pawn was redeemed, particularly among the dwellers of Santo Domingo Pueblo, considered among the most conservative and tradition-bound of all New Mexico pueblos. If it didn't fall victim to the onslaught of buyers and traders before the 1950s, where is it today?

Much authentic pawn jewelry was buried with the deceased Indian owner, particularly among the Navajo, fearful of the spirit of the dead. Callously taking pawn jewelry, the dead man's proudest possession, was considered irreverent.

To the Navajo there was only one alternative to burying the dead's jewelry. The pieces belonging to the deceased were washed in soap and water then pollen was sprinkled over them. On the first night after the burial, the jewelry was placed next to the appointed heir and chants were recited over the jewelry and the heir. On the second night, the Blessing Way ritual was sung and prayers offered. Then the heir could wear the jewelry without fear of spirits coming to return the jewelry to the deceased.

Even before pawn became part of the Pueblo economic system, turquoise and silver were part of the barter system among the White Mountain and Jicarilla Apaches, Navajo, Ute, Havasupai, Walapai and the pueblos of Isleta, Zia, Acoma, Laguna, Zuni, Hopi, and Santo Domingo. Variations of silver and turquoise barter later turned up at the pueblos of Taos, Jémez, Santa Clara and Santa Ana. Those would rank as antiquities, but not necessarily as old pawn.

Antique New Mexico silver and turquoise jewelry — authenticated as closely as possible — is now found at museums. Some public collections are at the Museum of New Mexico, Santa Fe; Museum of Northern Arizona, Flagstaff; Maxwell Museum, Albuquerque; Millicent Rogers Museum, Taos; and the Heard Museum, Phoenix.

For trader Fred Thompson and his wife, Alicia, life and business just aren't the same at Santo Domingo Indian Trading Post. Alicia remembers the early days when her sheepherder father, Everardo Montoya, would bring her from Peña Blanca to the post as a little girl to marvel at the Indian pawn.

All that has changed, but Thompson and Alicia have been there since 1950, open for customers. The post once was an important center for commerce for Peña Blanca, and the pueblos of San Felipe, Cochití and Santo Domingo.

The trading post, which was built in 1890, began losing business in 1932 when U.S. 85, now Interstate 25, bypassed it by about four miles; the Santa Fe Railway stop across the road no longer exists.

Crumbled adobe down the way attests to an era when the trading post was the center for a population of 1,500. When the winds howl at night, one's mind plays games, hearing the faint voices of ghosts of yesteryear, the whistles of a steam engine pulling into the station — a dirge for a lost era.

(Editor's Note: Fred Thompson died in 1994, shortly after being interviewed for this story. The Santo Domingo Trading post closed after his death and the historic building was destroyed by a suspicious fire in February 2001.)

The late Jack Hartsfield was a former business magazine editor, investigative journalist and free-lance writer based in Santa Fe.

This display at the Turquoise Museum, "Zack's Mine," depicts a traditional mine entrance.

NEW MEXICO'S CROWN JEWEL
SHINES AT THE TURQUOISE MUSEUM

BY PATRICIA O'CONNOR

There is only one place in the world where you can see a piece of natural turquoise the size of a generous pancake, the color of the New Mexico sky on a dry summer afternoon and shaped like the father of our country's big-nosed profile.

"This is the George Washington stone," says Katy Lowry, co-proprietor of the Zach-Low Turquoise Museum in Albuquerque. It comes from the Kingman mine in Arizona, weighs 6,880 carats and measures 10 inches by 11 1/2 inches. "This was in a drawer somewhere," says Katy, one of the heirs-apparent to her father's extensive collection of natural turquoise.

Today J.C. Zachary Jr.'s stash — the largest private collection in the world, say the Lowrys, is on permanent display in the world's first Turquoise Museum at 2107 Central NW in the Old Town Shopping Center, across Río Grande Boulevard from Albuquerque's Old Town.

Walk in the unassuming storefront past the family's gift and flower shops to the turquoise mine shaft built by Katy's husband Joe and their son, Joe Dan Lowry. Joe Dan points out the veins of blue. That's where the bigger pieces come from. He indicates the spots that look more like punctuation marks. "That's where you get nuggets," he says.

The narrow shaft opens up into a room full of the treasures. Among the prized pieces is a 16-pound nugget from the Bisbee mine in Arizona the size and shape of a soccer ball and a blue deeper than the Santa Fe sky before a rain. "This is the largest high-grade nugget to come out of the Bisbee mine ever," says Joe Lowry. It's just one of several one-of-a-kind stones.

The collection features turquoise the color of jade, stones riddled with matrix or smooth as a robin's egg. There's turquoise from the Fox, Lone Mountain, Blue Gem, Lander Blue, Morenci and Cerrillos mines, to name a few. They have turquoise from around the world, including Iran (formerly Persia), China and Australia. Lowry drops more names than a starlet does at a producer's cocktail party. The Turquoise Museum represents more than 60 mines, four continents and six countries. The Lowrys are still adding to the displays.

"We don't know how much more (turquoise) is stashed in bank vaults all over the place," Lowry says. "I will be cataloging until I die." Perhaps even more stunning: Everything in the

room is 100 percent natural turquoise. That is no small statement, since, as the statistics say, only 10 percent of the stuff on the market is natural. It's enough to give any squash blossom hunter pause.

WHERE DID IT COME FROM?

One of Katy Lowry's earliest memories is of her father, J.C. "Zack" Zachary Jr., coming home from the mines lugging in piles of raw, natural turquoise. He and his buddies dumped mountains of the stuff on the living room floor. Katy, who was 6 years old at the time, watched as the men licked and pinched the stones to see how they might look when they were cut and polished.

Above: This 2,620-carat stone on display at the museum was mined at Carico Lake near Crescent Valley, Nevada, and measures 4-inches by 3-inches by 1¾-inches.

Below: Natural turquoise ready to cut is glued on sticks in this exhibition at the Turquoise Museum.

"He used to tell us when we were growing up, 'This turquoise isn't going to be around for long. So many of these mines are shutting down,'" Katy remembers. Zack set aside his favorite stones in drawers and boxes and closet shelves. Turquoise was everywhere in the house, she remembers. "We didn't know what we had."

True to his prediction, mine after famous mine shut down. Sometimes they closed because the copper or gold ran out. Others closed because the next generation didn't want to take over the mom-and-pop mine. Subsequently, new governmental safety standards make mining more complicated and, consequently, too expensive for some old families to run. For whatever reason, turquoise mines closed and Zack's stash became rare and valuable.

Katy and Joe started their own wholesale turquoise shop in Albuquerque 25 years ago and kept some of Zack's cache in a vault. Word got out and turquoise fanciers started visiting. The Albuquerque Museum got wind of the collection and asked to display it as part of the "Facets: Gems and Minerals" exhibit from 1989 to 1991. One Airstream RV tour group asked if they could have a tour and training on the subject while blowing through town during

Above: The row of stones on the right illustrates (from bottom to top) low grade to high-grade Persian (Iranian) turquoise. The row on the left shows low-grade to high-grade (bottom to top) domestic turquoise stones from the Fox Mine in Nevada. Persian stones are used to guage turquoise quality worldwide. Under this standard, clear unblemished stones are considered of the highest quality and turquoise with matrix patterns are deemed lower grade.

Below: The Turquoise Museum also boasts the 6,880-carat George Washington Stone, a 10-inch by 11½-inch nugget of Turquoise Mountain turquoise from Kingman, Arizona.

the Albuquerque International Balloon Fiesta in 1989 and they've been coming back every year since. Such zeal for Zack's collection gave Katy an idea: Why not create our own turquoise museum? And that's just what they did in 1994.

The idea to create a museum might not have occurred to Katy had she not witnessed her father's passion for the stone when she was a little girl. She remembers sneaking into the living room after her father and his friends left for lunch. She and her baby brother, Bob, carefully licked every stone in the pile as a surprise for her dad. Of course, by the time they returned, the stones were dry and looked just the same as when he left.

Left: Marion Nez creates jewelry at Zachary Turquoise Inc., located behind the museum.

Opposite: These sterling-silver bookends at the Turquoise Museum are adorned with natural turquoise from Kingman.

"That's what gave me the taste for turquoise," she jokes. "I tell people now I have turquoise in my blood."

BLUE BLOODS

The Zachary branch of the family tree has dabbled in the turquoise trade since the early 1930s when J.C. Zachary Sr. began trading in the Navajo Nation. In 1935, he moved to southern Colorado to manage the now-famous Villa Grove Turquoise Mine.

Katy's father started cutting turquoise at age 9. He took to the trade like he was born to it, which he was. In 1945 he opened his own turquoise shop specializing in natural turquoise. Zack's son, Bob, joined him and they ran Zachary Turquoise Inc.

In the meantime, Katy and her husband, Joe Lowry, opened their own wholesale turquoise business, Zach-Low, Inc. Their son, Joe Dan, now carries the blue/green baton. He gives most of the tours and educational lectures at the museum.

Joe Dan gets his gift for educational banter from his father. Since 1969, Joe has given educational seminars to folks in the industry. In 1979, he was invited to speak at a meeting of the National Indian Arts and Crafts Association. That talk turned into an article for *Indian Trader Magazine*. Since then, he has been invited by the National Park Concessionaires at Carlsbad Caverns, the Grand Canyon and Yellowstone National Park, among others, to give seminars to their staffs. Representatives from the Smithsonian Museum and the New Mexico and Arizona attorney-general offices have signed up for the talk.

You might say the Lowrys are on a mission: "To preserve the largest collection of rare, natural turquoise specimens in the world while providing consumer education," Katy reads from the museum's mission statement. In short, the Zach-Low Turquoise Museum is more than just a pretty place.

ALL THAT GLITTERS ...

Historically speaking, turquoise tales abound. According to some Native American traditions, for example, turquoise has protective powers. "You can tell who's wearing real turquoise on the golf course during a lightning storm," Joe Dan says. "They're the guys who keep playing. The ones wearing fakes run inside."

Mother lodes of myths and misinformation about turquoise are even more prevalent, the Lowrys say. Buyers not only must beware but they better know the lingo, Joe Dan says. Don't be fooled by turns of phrase, such as "Indian handcrafted" or "Indian assembled," he says. That might refer to the piecing together of machine-made settings. Even a signature on the back might be stamped by a machine. If you want to see authentic handmade silverwork in action, keep walking through the museum. Bob Zachary's living lapidary shop is set up in the back behind glass where Native American artists cut stones and set them using machines built by Zachary.

Also beware of turquoise that's labeled "genuine" or "real," Joe Dan says. "There are only two things you need to know," he says. "Is it natural and is it authentic Indian handmade? These are the only two descriptions recognized by law."

To help people understand the difference, the Lowrys give educational seminars. All the tours of the museum are self-guided, so people can learn what interests them most. Some folks come in with a newly purchased piece of turquoise around their necks and sweat on their brow. The Lowrys won't appraise. Nor will they tell people if it's fake. However, they do strongly suggest that when you buy, ask for a letter of authenticity.

To help consumers know their turquoise, the Turquoise Museum features displays of everything from the pure and natural to the oiled, dyed and plastic. One case features plastic and natural stones together. The challenge is if you can tell the difference. "Experts can identify fake turquoise about 80 percent of the time," Joe Dan says. Don't feel bad if you don't guess right the first time.

Education being the cornerstone of the Lowrys' operation, Joe and Joe Dan avail themselves to give interactive seminars on or off site. On site, they charge a nominal per-person fee, which includes a tour of the museum. Off site, the Lowrys charge more but they add an IOU for a visit to the museum.

"People come to New Mexico to buy turquoise. We give them an opportunity to find out what's out there so they don't leave here with a bad taste in their mouths," Katy says. And she knows from experience that once you've gotten a taste for natural turquoise there's no going back.

Patricia O'Connor, an Albuquerque-based free lance writer, is a regular contributor to *New Mexico Magazine* and has published her work in *Southwest Airlines* magazine and *Art of the West*.

1. Kingman, AZ
2. Stormy Mountain, NV
3. Kingman, AZ
4. Stabilized
5. Concho Springs, NV
6. Waxed
7. Stabilized
8. Waxed
9. Stabilized
10. Fox, NV
11. Concho Springs, NV
12. Stormy Mountain, NV
13. Morenci, AZ
14. Kingman, AZ
15. Sleeping Beauty, AZ
16. Sleeping Beauty, AZ
17. Waxed
18. Stabilized
19. Stabilized
20. Waxed
21. Stabilized
22. Persian (Iran)
23. Persian (Iran)
24. Lone Mountain, NV
25. Blue Gem, NV
26. Kingman, AZ
27. Morenci, AZ
28. Color Shot
29. Waxed
30. Fracture Sealed
31. Fracture Sealed
32. Stabilized
33. Barredo, NV
34. Kingman, AZ
35. Fox, NV
36. Morenci, AZ
37. Kingman, AZ
38. Manassa Green, CO
39. Tyrone, NM
40. Waxed
41. Enhanced
42. Royston, NV
43. Sky Horse, China
44. Plastic
45. Kingman, AZ
46. Warm Springs, NV

This conglomerate compiled by the Turquoise Museum in Albuquerque illustrates various turquoise stones.

Inside the Tiffany Mine, Douglas Magnus points to a vein structure typical of the type that once was mined there for turquoise. Although there are no current mining operations at Tiffany, Magnus is working to preserve the mine for future generations. (Photo by Steve Voynick)

JEWELER STRIVES TO PRESERVE CERRILLOS MINES

BY STEVE VOYNICK

As Doug Magnus and I slowly make our way up the hillside on a warm spring morning, the only sound is the scraping of our boots against broken rock. "This hill is mostly altered volcanic rock," Magnus explains quietly. "But if you look closely, you'll find some turquoise — like this piece right here."

Magnus reaches down, picks up what seems to be a pebble, and hands it to me. Initially, I see only a nondescript, half-inch long stone the color of iron rust. But when I turn it over, I'm startled by a narrow vein of blue that is even brighter than the sky overhead.

"That intense, clean blue is typical of Tiffany Cerrillos turquoise," Magnus says. "Turquoise doesn't come any better than this." Most of the other turquoise produced in the area has more of a greenish hue to it.

Magnus, a Santa Fe jewelry maker and belt-buckle designer, knows and loves Cerrillos turquoise better than anyone. And his interest goes beyond the gemstone's beauty to the Cerrillos turquoise mines themselves — mines that have produced what is arguably the most beautiful, and without question, the most historically significant turquoise, ever found in the United States.

Magnus owns three of the most fabled of these mines — the Tiffany, the Castilian and the Alicia. And today it is the Tiffany Mine that appears before us as an ominously deep, sheer-walled open pit.

We are standing on Turquoise Hill, a low ridge at the edge of the Cerrillos Hills (mining) District, just a 25-minute drive south of Santa Fe. Of the dozen or so turquoise sources that lie scattered through the Cerrillos Hills, the Tiffany, Castilian and Alicia mines have been among the most productive.

"Pueblo Indians began mining turquoise here about A.D. 600," Magnus tells me. "They traded much of it to the Chaco Canyon culture in northwestern New Mexico. Many Southwestern native cultures considered Cerrillos turquoise a sacred stone. It was so widely traded that archaeologists have found it at sites throughout much of North America."

Pueblo Indians were still mining turquoise at Turquoise Hill when the Spanish arrived in the early 1600s. For the next 50 years, while the Spanish mined lead and silver in the Cerrillos Hills, the Puebloans continued to mine turquoise. But after the Pueblo Revolt of 1680 abruptly ended this peaceful coexistence, mining was never the same again, even after peace was restored.

During the 1700s and even later, when the region fell under Mexican rule in 1821, scattered bands of Puebloans mined turquoise only occasionally. Then in 1879, three decades after the region became part of the United States, American miners began exploiting the silver and lead deposits once worked by the Spanish.

But because turquoise then had little demand or value as a gemstone, these miners ignored the nearby, ancient deposits, leaving them to the few Pueblo Indians who continued to dig for the sky-blue and green stones. Nevertheless, in 1880, the Cerrillos Hills District provided almost all the turquoise mined in the United States. Its estimated value? A mere $2,000.

"But in the mid-1880s, companies began promoting turquoise in big East Coast markets," Magnus says. "Prestigious jewelers like Tiffany & Co. got into the act, and art nouveau gold jewelry, soon grew enormously popular." The combination of turquoise and silver jewelry came into fashion, he says, primarily when the Fred Harvey Company began promoting the Southwest and encouraged Indians to sell jewelry and other crafts at railroad stops in the early 1900s.

As turquoise became much more valuable, American miners began working the old diggings with modern equipment and dynamite. By the 1890s, they were turning out nearly a quarter-million dollars worth of fine turquoise each year.

"Putting things into historical perspective," Magnus notes, "it was Cerrillos turquoise that established the popularity of turquoise as a gemstone in the United States."

Shortly after the turn of the century, the Cerrillos Hills turquoise deposits, now largely exhausted, faced growing competition from new Southwestern turquoise mines. Regular production faded out about 1910, after which the mines were visited only sporadically by Native American miners, Anglo prospectors, treasure hunters, and mineral and artifact collectors.

In the early 1970s, Magnus, then an aspiring jewelry designer, was one of the few people who still collected Cerrillos turquoise. "I've never forgotten my first visit to the Cerrillos mines," Magnus recalls. "I was captivated both by the beauty of the panorama from atop Turquoise Hill and by the abundant evidence of early mining — trenches, piles of rubble, deep pits, collapsing portals and bits of turquoise scattered everywhere. As I began researching the history of the mines, I realized that Cerrillos — both the gemstone and the mines — was very special."

Above: Among the artifacts that Magnus has found on the Tiffany Mine property is this stone maul, which was used by Pueblo Indians centuries ago to mine turquoise.

Below: The view from the Tiffany Mine looking southward toward the Cerrillos Hills. *Cerro* is the Spanish word for hills, thus the town name. (Photos by Steve Voynick)

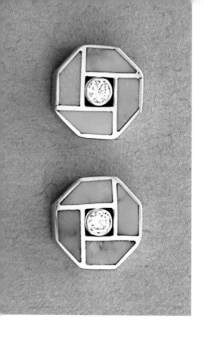

In 1985, Magnus was already known as one of Santa Fe's top silver belt-buckle and silver-and-turquoise jewelry designers. That same year, he heard rumors that someone was selling Cerrillos turquoise from a mine site. Visiting the old Tiffany Mine, he found a ramshackle camp where a caretaker-prospector lived with his family. For several years, this prospector had scraped out a meager living by digging, cutting and selling Cerrillos turquoise.

"I bought some rough turquoise at a bargain price," Magnus remembers. "And I also became intrigued by the mines themselves."

Magnus first arranged to lease the 10-acre Castilian Mine site and began digging small amounts of

Above: These earrings made in 2002 feature diamonds and Cerrillos turquoise.

Below: Cerrillos turquoise and diamonds accentuate these ornamental earrings made in 2004. (Photos courtesy of Douglas Magnus/Heartline)

turquoise. Shortly afterward, the owners of the Tiffany and Castilian mines put the properties up for sale — and Magnus was first in line to buy them. Magnus ultimately became the principal owner of all three of the historic turquoise mines, including the Alicia mine.

"Although the biggest pieces of turquoise had been mined long ago," Magnus explains, "owning the mines gave me access to a small, but steady supply of small pieces of Cerrillos turquoise. So I began making turquoise jewelry, creating designs that maximized the use of these small pieces. My goal was to make Cerrillos turquoise jewelry available again — even if only in the Santa Fe area — for the first time in decades."

Magnus even developed a new line of jewelry

— his top-of-the-line "Castilian Collection"
— that matches Cerrillos turquoise with gold,
diamonds and pearls. Beyond cutting and
polishing, his Cerrillos turquoise — unlike much
other turquoise on the market — is never altered,
treated or color-enhanced in any way.

We squeeze through a small, timbered
portal and into a low, narrow tunnel where just
enough daylight enables us to avoid rough rock
protruding from the walls. Some 50 feet into the
tunnel, a heavy, locked steel gate blocks the way.
While opening the padlock, Magnus explains
that this gate, as well as the high, chain-link
fences enclosing all the surface pits, were installed

Above: Turquoise from Cerrillos and diamonds highlight this gold necklace made in 2001.

Below: The pieces of Cerrillos turquoise in this necklace made in 2003 present variety of blue and green hues. (Photos courtesy of Douglas Magnus/Heartline)

in 1999 as part of a statewide, mined-land
reclamation program to make old mine workings
safe.

"This is the main Tiffany Mine,"
Magnus says as we make our way deeper into
the underground. "American miners drove this
particular tunnel in the 1900s. But we're coming
to workings that are much, much older."

The tunnel soon grows brighter and we
emerge into the bottom of a bowl-like vertical
excavation. Fifty feet above us the surface rim,
part of a juniper tree, and the blue New Mexico
sky become visible.

"Notice how the upper walls are smooth,"

Above left: Tiny squares of Cerrillos turquoise arranged in a mosaic pattern make this 2002 necklace interesting.

Above right: Turquoise from Cerrillos cut in geometrical patterns hint of modern design in this champagne diamond necklace. (Photos courtesy of Douglas Magnus/Heartline)

Magnus points out. "That work was done centuries ago by Puebloan miners who used heavy stone mauls to literally pound the rock apart. But see how the lower walls are rough and jagged? That's where American miners drilled and blasted the rock in the 1890s.

"There is very little visible turquoise here," he continues. "It was all cleaned out by miners, mineral collectors and treasure hunters long before I bought the mines. There may be more turquoise veins within the rock, but I doubt we'll ever know for sure. Environmental constraints and high costs rule out any attempts at mechanized mining that might reveal additional veins. So it's unlikely these mines will ever produce turquoise again. Nevertheless, they are historically and culturally invaluable."

So what will Magnus do with his old turquoise mines? "For the time being, I'll retain ownership to protect them from subdivision and development, and from being filled in, built

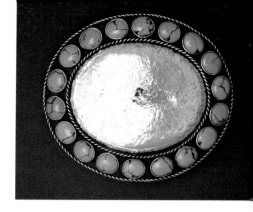

From top to bottom: Magnus/Heartline incorporated turquoise from China in this sterling sliver concho buckle made in 2004.

Natural Chinese turquoise and sterling silver highlight this bracelet made in 2004.

Stabilized turquoise from a mine in Kingman, Ariz., decorates this fanciful bracelet made in 2002.

Intricately placed pieces of Chinese turquoise bring this 2004 sterling silver bracelet to life. (Photos courtesy of Douglas Magnus/Heartline)

on, and forgotten," he says. "And eventually, I'll leave them to an appropriate organization, perhaps the University of New Mexico or the Archaeological Conservancy, both of which are in nearby Albuquerque. I want to be assured that the mines will always be available for historical, archaeological and mineralogical study."

Magnus picks up another small piece of turquoise and smiles. "Countless craftsmen have worked Cerrillos turquoise for a thousand years, and I guess I'm the last of that long line," he concludes. "So I've made it my job to see that these mines and all that they represent are preserved for the future."

Based in Twin Lakes, Colo., Steve Voynick is the author of 10 books, several on the subject of mining and gemstones. He visited more than 150 mining and collecting sites throughout the state to research and write *New Mexico Rockhounding.*

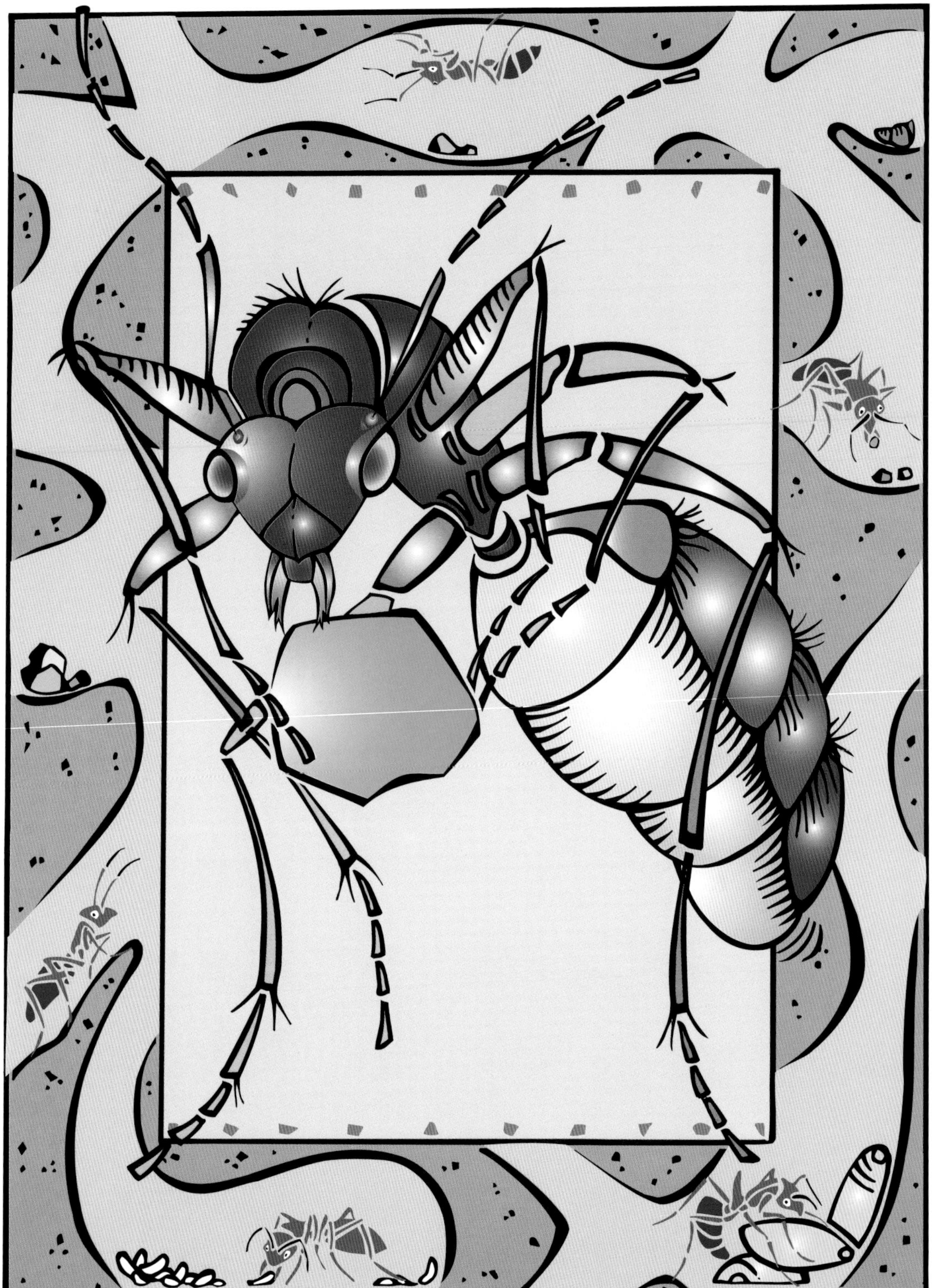

ANTS AND TURQUOISE: A DISCERNING RELATIONSHIP

BY SUSAN ARRITT

The most voracious turquoise collectors in New Mexico pay no mind to laws prohibiting removal of artifacts from prehistoric ruin sites. En masse, they go about their raids in broad daylight, and often dig tunnels to unearth long-buried, ancient turquoise beads.

Masters at the art of excavation, the collectors can single-handedly lug away loads of the gemstone that far exceed their own weight. These avid gatherers that accomplish feats not humanly possible are, in fact, harvester ants, truly the "antaeologists" of the archaeological world.

Throughout many regions of the Southwest it is not uncommon to spot all sorts of collected debris and objects poking out of or lying atop anthills, or "nests." But passersby tempted by artifacts — like bones, potsherds, tiny awls, or beads of turquoise or other stones — are wise to heed a word of warning: Both species of harvester ants native to New Mexico — the dark brown or black *Pogonomyrmex rugosus* and the reddish-orange *Pogonomyrmex occidentalis*, or western harvester ant — are legendary for debilitating stings that deliver some of the most toxic venom of all insects.

Some archaeologists believe that, although such ant activity can give clues to underground artifacts at ruin sites, it nearly always leads to detrimental contamination and skewing of the cultural record. But National Park Service archaeologist Thomas Windes had a feeling decades ago that harvester ants could actually play a vital role in his studies at Chaco Canyon. There, turquoise was a tremendously important mineral in prehistoric times, as evidenced by the 56,000 pieces — mostly in the form of beads and pendants — that were found in Pueblo Bonito during an 1890s dig. Deciphering the turquoise collecting behaviors of the ants in the region, Windes strongly contends, is one roundabout way to get a better understanding of how human residents lived there a thousand years ago.

Since 1976, for example, when he first mapped all the ant nests at one ruin site, Windes has been fascinated by the fact that harvester ants have an affinity for turquoise. The insects are not keen on just any old stone, Windes says, but have a penchant for blue and green ones in particular. Windes knows that for a fact, because, as an offshoot of his work in the Park Service's Chaco Project, he actually tested the bead color preferences of harvester ants in the canyon. Several hundred identically sized, glass beads colored red, orange, yellow, green, blue, clear and black were placed at distances ranging from nine to 30 feet away from four ant nests. Over a three-year period, Windes observed the fate of the beads.

"We've never recovered all of them," he says. "Some of them are still buried out there, where the rains have covered them up by dirt. And some probably got blasted to space by raindrops." Five years after his study began, Windes still watches out for the missing beads when he goes to the same ant nests at a ruin site in Chaco Canyon. He has found a sufficient number of the beads to conclude statistically that blue and green — the natural colors of gem-quality turquoise — are far and away the colors of choice for harvester ants.

Most turquoise fragments found at an ant nest coat the outside of the structure's dome, like a roofing veneer. The fragments are usually so small they would sift through the typical quarter-inch sieve and be missed during a typical archaeological dig. Windes postulates that ants choose turquoise over stones of other colors because of some sort of thermal properties afforded by the blue and green stone. "Earlier ant literature said ants were color-blind," he says. "But it's been demonstrated that they respond to the blue-green spectrum." Windes is "more convinced now that it's a solar kind of thing," and thinks that perhaps turquoise "acts as a thermal collector — open in summer, closed in winter," and that the ants are "trying to maintain a standard temperature" year-round in their nests.

His ultimate aim is not to figure out ants, but to see what correlation lies between their turquoise collections and nearby ruin sites. "Blue-green is a color that (ants) recognize in some way," Windes says, "but more importantly, I'm understanding their behavior — how far they'll go to pick up stuff and when they're more likely to grab it and bring it on the nest. I want to know the association between sites and nearby ant houses.

"All I knew is that, back in the old days, the ants were getting all my turquoise," Windes remarks. "I had to understand more about ant behavior to understand some of the artifact distribution on the sites. How far will an ant go to collect stuff? I didn't have the slightest idea. How long would ants live? How long have these mounds been around? When you're looking at the ant nest and they've got turquoise on it, and the ant nest is about 50 meters away, how can I say that turquoise came from that shrine? What is the relationship between the ant nest and the cultural aspect that's around them?"

Right: Ants latch on to tiny pieces of turquoise near their nest. Just like humans, harvester ants throughout the Southwest have a special relationship with turquoise.

In 1976, Windes led the full-scale excavation of a small-house site near Fajada Butte in Chaco Canyon. A tremendous amount of turquoise turned up on the site and most was on or around 19 local ant nests. The thousands of blue-green fragments indicated that major ornament production took place at that small-house during the early Chacoan period, which lasted from the late A.D. 900s to early A.D. 1000s. Accurately knowing the relationship between that one ruin and its turquoise-laden ant nests has enabled Windes to reliably predict the extent of human activities — like jewelry manufacturing — at other sites by surveying the turquoise caches in their resident ant nests. The ants "are essentially doing my mining for me," he says, and are saving him the trouble and expense of having to do full-scale excavations at every site.

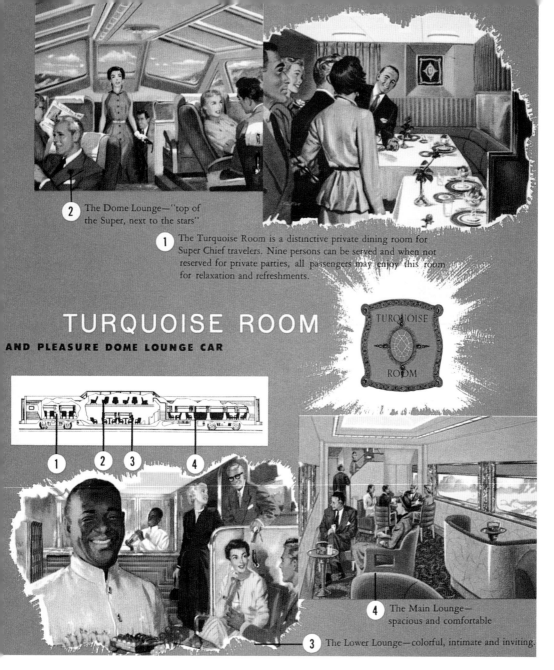

2 The Dome Lounge—"top of the Super, next to the stars".

1 The Turquoise Room is a distinctive private dining room for Super Chief travelers. Nine persons can be served and when not reserved for private parties, all passengers may enjoy this room for relaxation and refreshments.

TURQUOISE ROOM
AND PLEASURE DOME LOUNGE CAR

TURQUOISE ROOM

4 The Main Lounge— spacious and comfortable

3 The Lower Lounge—colorful, intimate and inviting.

The Pleasure Dome lounge car on the 1951 Super Chief was one of the most luxurious cars ever made for any train. The most famous innovation in this car was the first private dining room on rails, the Turquoise Room. It could be reserved any time, day or night, for private parties or any other special event. When not in use, other passengers could enjoy the ambiance of this special room. This spread is from an early 1950s Super Chief brochure.

Graphics in this chapter courtesy of John Vaughan from his book, *Santa Fe, The Chief Way*, published by *New Mexico Magazine*.

SENTIMENTAL JOURNEYS OF THE TURQUOISE ROOM

BY RAY NELSON

The resounding blast of the Super Chief's air horn no longer echoes across the canyons and hills of New Mexico.

The famous red and silver train has faded into history, and now The Land of Enchantment is crisscrossed with high-altitude jet contrails, 75 mph interstates and, of course, Amtrak. But for those who rode on the elegant flagship train of the Santa Fe Railway, it was an unforgettable travel experience.

The Super Chief, billed by Santa Fe as the train that sets a new world standard in travel, was a "grand hotel on rails." It offered daily service between Chicago and Los Angeles, crossing the country at speeds of up to 90 mph and averaging 60. A special feature of the Super Chief was its Pleasure Dome lounge car containing an observation dome, a spacious main lounge, a comfortable lower lounge and the Turquoise Room, an intimate private dining room that seated up to 10 people.

This unique dining room embodied the elegance and grandeur of mid-century train travel on the Santa Fe. It was 120 square feet of unrivaled luxury, "All the luxury of dining at your favorite night club," said a Santa Fe Railway ad. "For its size, this is the most famous restaurant in the world," proclaimed a Santa Fe promotional poster. "Transcontinental commuters love the feeling of a private club enroute that the Turquoise Room gives them."

The Turquoise Room was available at no extra charge for private dinners, afternoon cocktail parties and even birthday parties. It was also opened for overflow dining in case the main dining car was full. Gold-hued fabric, natural wood and sand paintings decorated the walls, while recorded dinner music set the right mood. At one end of the dining room was a large oval-shaped medallion made of inlaid turquoise and mounted on a background of black velvet with a frame of silver and turquoise. The medallion was appropriate for passengers making the 2,267-mile, cross-country journey because turquoise is considered the traveler's stone throughout the world.

An advertisement for the Super Chief that appeared in national magazines included a color photograph of sophisticated, well-dressed passengers seated at dinner tables with white

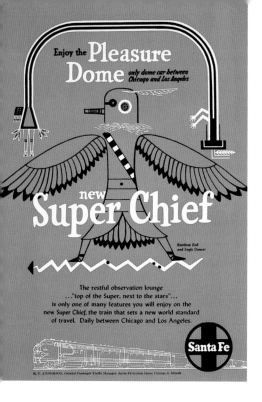

Enjoy the **Pleasure Dome** *only dome car between Chicago and Los Angeles*

new **Super Chief**

Rainbow God and Eagle Dancer

The restful observation lounge ..."top of the Super, next to the stars"... is only one of many features you will enjoy on the new *Super Chief*, the train that sets a new world standard of travel. Daily between Chicago and Los Angeles.

Santa Fe

R. T. ANDERSON, General Passenger Traffic Manager, Santa Fe System Lines, Chicago 4, Illinois

linen tablecloths, special Turquoise Room service plates and large Turquoise Room menus featuring a drawing of the wall medallion on the cover. On the back of the menu it said, "This room symbolizes the colorful Indian country of the Southwest where turquoise is both a sacred talisman and a symbol of wealth and prosperity."

The menu featured *a la carte* selections from the adjacent Fred Harvey dining car, entrees such as grilled Canadian whitefish, *Maitre d'Hotel* at $2.20 (in 1964), roast rack of spring lamb, natural gravy, mint jelly at $2.10 and charcoal-broiled sirloin steak at $7.75, plus California table wine, and a fine selection of appetizers, soups, salads and desserts.

Above: The Rainbow God and Eagle Dancer motifs are used in this ad to promote the Pleasure Dome lounge car on the new 1951 Super Chief.

Below: This ad appeared in *National Geographic* in 1951 to announce the new Super Chief when it was completely re-equipped with new cars.

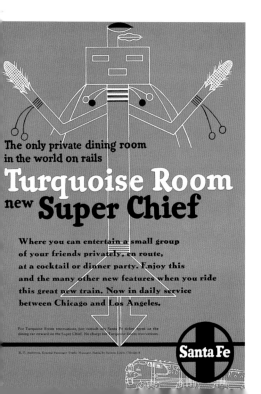

The only private dining room in the world on rails

Turquoise Room new **Super Chief**

Where you can entertain a small group of your friends privately, en route, at a cocktail or dinner party. Enjoy this and the many other new features when you ride this great new train. Now in daily service between Chicago and Los Angeles.

For Turquoise Room reservations, just consult any Santa Fe ticket agent or the dining car steward on the Super Chief. No charge for Turquoise Room reservations.

Santa Fe

R. T. Anderson, General Passenger Traffic Manager, Santa Fe System Lines, Chicago 4, Illinois

Railroad writer Stan Repp said the Turquoise Room offered matchless fare and impeccable service. In a May 1962 issue of *Trains* magazine, Repp wrote that at dinner on the Super Chief's first night out, passengers who wanted fresh trout for dinner the next day placed their orders with the chef, who then wired ahead to the Fred Harvey Creamery in Las Vegas, N.M. Fresh-caught trout were picked up when the Super Chief reached Las Vegas at 1:35 p.m. westbound or 4:52 p.m. eastbound.

Jon Messier, of Albuquerque, recalls dining in the Turquoise Room as a boy of 12 when traveling to California. He remembers that the room was very impressive, with striking decor that really captured all

In the Turquoise Room . .

"REALLY LIVING"
a la Super Chief

Extra Fare — and worth it!

All private room streamlined train between Chicago-Los Angeles

This full-page ad for the Super Chief says it all. Luxurious surroundings and outstanding food were the hallmarks of this famous streamliner.

A full-page ad for all three of the major Santa Fe trains in the mid-1950s. The famous Turquoise Room of the Super Chief is shown at the top.

Above: The Hi-Level El Capitan speeds through New Mexico's Shoemaker Canyon.

Below: This baggage tag from the 1937 Super Chief shows the stylized Indian motif used during the '30s and '40s.

the romance of the Southwest and particularly New Mexico. "It was just awe-inspiring to be in such an elegant dining room and travel at up to 90 miles an hour and eat foods you never thought you would eat!" Messier got to dine in the Turquoise Room again in the early 1970s on a trip to San Diego, after Amtrak took over, and this time he had his 4-year-old son with him. He recalls that it was still very nice, but not like the days of the Super Chief.

After 1976 the Pleasure Dome lounge cars of the Super Chief began to be taken out of service, with the last one being sold in 1980. There were six of these, one for each of the six Super Chief trains in use.

Ray Nelson, an Albuquerque-based free-lance writer, is a frequent contributor to *New Mexico Magazine*.

Sandía Crest and the Manzano Mountains in the far background illuminate in the late afternoon sunlight.

THE TURQUOISE TRAIL REMAINS TIMELESS

BY EMILY DRABANSKI

It wasn't only the lure of turquoise. Gold, coal and silver also once enticed
adventurous spirits to the rough-and-tumble towns of Golden, Cerrillos and Madrid.

Today, the lure of spectacular terrain, as well as the mystique of historic mining towns,
brings folks out along what is now called the Turquoise Trail on N.M. 14. This scenic winding
back road between Albuquerque and Santa Fe offers a glimpse into the past.

Along the way, you'll have a chance to stop for refreshments at quiet cafes or lively
taverns. Modern treasure hunters can browse through antique shops and galleries. You might
even find silver and turquoise — in some of the stores on your journey.

The Turquoise Trail Association, a group representing businesses along the route,
suggests beginning your tour by getting off Interstate 40 east of Albuquerque at the exit to
Cedar Crest and N.M. 14.

Cedar Crest and Sandía Park offer mountain terrain on the east side of the Sandía
Mountains. Albuquerque residents often take a cruise to dine at several popular restaurants in
the tall pines or just to take a Sunday drive.

At the Sandía Crest turnoff, you can venture off N.M. 14 to N.M. 536 to take a
breathtaking ride to the summit along the Sandía Crest National Scenic Byway. In the summer
bring your hiking boots to find a cool respite in the towering ponderosa pine. En route stop
at the Tinkertown Miniature Village, just a mile from the turnoff. The miniature Old West
town is open from April through October. The glass bottle walls glisten in the sunlight and
surround a potter's studio and gift shop.

Downhill and cross-country skiers will find a winter wonderland at the Sandia Peak Ski
Area. In the summer you can take a heart-pounding ride on the chair lifts. Six miles farther
you'll reach the crest with breathtaking views at 10,678 feet. At this vantage point you might
spot golden eagles as they soar over the crest. From the observation deck, you can see more
than 15,000 square miles encompassing deserts, mountains and volcanoes.

Stretch your legs on the hiking trails in the mountain terrain, which is a part of the
Cíbola National Forest. Walk through the forest, home to Rocky Mountain bighorn sheep,

mule deer and a variety of birds. Afterward, you might want to browse through the shop or get a bite to eat at the restaurant at the crest before beginning your descent.

As you leave the cutoff and head north on N.M. 14, the terrain changes near the foothills of the Ortíz Mountains. Junipers, piñon, sage and cholla cactus punctuate the roadside as you approach a mineral-rich area that once supported three booming mine towns.

Golden, named for a gold rush in the latter 1800s, once boasted saloons and a stock exchange. Now, Golden's most famous landmark is a small church resting quietly among the cholla cactus.

About eight miles down the road is Madrid with its rows of old, wooden frame houses. Coal, an important fuel in the 1880s, led to the growth of this town. Following World War II the coal demand lessened, leading to the collapse and abandonment of the town.

In the 1950s, the owner tried to sell the whole town and had no takers. In the mid-'70s, he sold off the houses individually. He sold them for a song, although there was hardly anything left to hum about. The old frame houses had dilapidated roofs and were missing walls. But a lot of sweat, hammers and nails have restored a number of homes — many filled with folks seeking an alternative lifestyle. Today, many of these buildings house interesting shops.

You can descend into an old mine shaft at the Old Coal Mine Museum and see mining relics sprawled across a few acres. Old movie projectors, telephone boxes and mining tools

Above: A row of wooden frame houses line the street in Madrid. (Historical photo by Loring W. Spitler, Museum of New Mexico Negative No. 53291)

Opposite: The Mine Shaft Tavern in Madrid. (Photo by Terry Tiedeman)

give a fascinating glimpse into the past. Youngsters and the young-at-heart will enjoy climbing aboard the old 1900 steam locomotive on the grounds.

Adjacent is the Mine Shaft Tavern, serving spirits, food and entertainment with the flavor of an Old West saloon. The Engine House Theatre offers productions in the adjacent space. In the summer, melodramas attract crowds that boo and hiss at the villains. Across the road there's a snack and gift shop in an old train car.

Many of Madrid's residents sell arts and crafts. The former company store, which dominates the main drag, now houses several shops along a wooden boardwalk. You'll find imported clothing and an eclectic mix of furniture and handcrafted wares. In other stores in town, you can often watch jewelers, potters, leatherworkers and weavers as they work at their crafts.

Years ago, the old ballpark had one of the hottest teams in the state when the miners got to bat. Nowadays, the field sometimes fills with dancers and music lovers who kick back to enjoy jazz, blues and bluegrass concerts in the summer.

In the 1920s and '30s, Madrid was well-known for its spectacular light displays at Christmas. Airline pilots would reroute their courses just to show off the site. In modern times, the community generally has a holiday open house on the weekends before Christmas.

Above: The streets of Cerrillos were used in the movies *Young Guns* and *Wyatt Earp*. (Photo by Terry Tiedeman)

Opposite: The Turquoise Hills near the entrance to the Tiffany Mine bask in the last sunrays of the day.

Hot chocolate and cider, along with carolers await visitors. At night, holiday lights twinkle.

Several miles from Madrid is Cerrillos (Spanish for little hills). Here, turquoise, gold, silver, lead, zinc as well as turquoise were extracted. In its heyday during the 1880s, the town had more than 20 saloons and four hotels. The Palace Hotel welcomed guests such as Thomas A. Edison, Ulysses S. Grant and Gov. L. Bradford Prince. Only rubble of the hotel remains.

Along with the town's prosperity came outlaws. It was the site of several shootouts. One of the more interesting tales involves a shootout over a madam. Evidently two miners had staked their claim on her charms.

Cerrillos still looks like an Old West movie set and indeed Hollywood has returned here many times to film. The movies *Young Guns* and *Wyatt Earp* as well as many others were shot in the area.

Many of the old buildings are private homes, but you're welcome to browse in the shops around town. You'll find antiques and an assortment of goods in the What-Not Shop. Another fun stop is the Casa Grande Trading Post. The funky trading post fills a 21-room adobe and includes a homegrown museum with information on turquoise mining. A small petting zoo is a favorite of the youngsters. As you leave town, a sign bids *"Hasta la Vista."*

North along N.M. 14, the Old West town fades in your memory as the hillsides are dotted with newer adobe and frame homes. A favorite stop for Santa Feans, as well as visitors is the San Marcos Cafe. Built next to a feed store, chickens and turkeys often wander in front of this laid-back country cafe.

The end of the Turquoise Trail will take you into Santa Fe. Otherwise return down N.M. 14 or take the faster route along Interstate 25 back to Albuquerque. When planning your trip, allow plenty of time. The winding two-lane road calls for alert driving.

A number of new cafes have appeared in recent years. But it's best to call first to determine hours. Also, for folks who want to spend more time, there are now several bed & breakfast establishments. For more information about businesses on the Turquoise Trail, write to the association at P.O. Box 303, Sandía Park, N.M. 87047; (505) 281-5233. www.turquoisetrail.org

Happy Trails to you!

Emily Drabanski is editor in chief of *New Mexico Magazine*. The Turquoise Trail is one of her favorite getaways.